WHITE COLLAR ZEN

WHITE COLLAR ZEN

Using Zen Principles to Overcome Obstacles and Achieve Your Career Goals

STEVEN HEINE

OXFORD
UNIVERSITY PRESS

2005

OXFORD
UNIVERSITY PRESS

Oxford University Press, Inc., publishes works that further
Oxford University's objective of excellence
in research, scholarship, and education.

Oxford   New York
Auckland   Cape Town   Dar es Salaam   Hong Kong   Karachi
Kuala Lumpur   Madrid   Melbourne   Mexico City   Nairobi
New Delhi   Shanghai   Taipei   Toronto

With offices in
Argentina   Austria   Brazil   Chile   Czech Republic   France   Greece
Guatemala   Hungary   Italy   Japan   Poland   Portugal   Singapore
South Korea   Switzerland   Thailand   Turkey   Ukraine   Vietnam

Copyright © 2005 by Oxford University Press

Published by Oxford University Press, Inc.
198 Madison Avenue, New York, New York 10016
www.oup.com

Oxford is a registered trademark of Oxford University Press

Library of Congress Cataloging-in-Publication Data
is available
ISBN-13: 978-0-19-516003-1
ISBN-10: 0-19-516003-7

1 3 5 7 9 8 6 4 2
Printed in the United States of America
on acid-free paper

Contents

PART THREE

Mountains Are Mountains Again:
From Structure to Anti-Structure

APPENDIX:

Koan Translation

Acknowledgments

SOME OF THE MATERIAL in this book has previously appeared in the following journal articles: "Ch'an Buddhist Kung-Ans as Models for Interpersonal Behavior," *Journal of Chinese Philosophy*, 30/3–4 (2003): 525–540; "Zen in the Workplace: Applying Anti-Structure to Enhance Structure," *Global Business Language*, 9 (2004); "Critical View of Discourses on the Relation between Japanese Business and Social Values," *Journal of Language for International Business*, 15/2 (2004). The picture on p. 38 of "Kuei-shan kicking over the water pitcher" appears courtesy of Ryoanji temple in Kyoto (it is also in Nishimura Eshin, ed., Mumonkan, Tokyo: Iwanami shoten, 1993). The statue of Pai-chang holding the fly-whisk on p. 113 is held at Saijoji temple (aka. Daiyuzan) near Odawara city.

White Collar Zen is dedicated to my Sensei, who sometimes pounded his fist so hard there was blood on the table. I will always remember those words we laughed out loud about as we waited in the parking lot of a 24-hour auto service mall one steamy summer night. May he rest.

This book could not have been written without tremendous support and assistance from the right persons. I especially thank

Cynthia Read of Oxford University Press, who believed in the project from the very beginning and went way beyond the call of duty at every step in editing the manuscript on multiple levels.

Several extremely insightful assistants helped the project, including Jessica Reyes and Melissa Sekkel. In addition, Cristina Sasso and Patricia Gonzalez were helpful, and there were additional comments on portions of the manuscript from Sandy Avila, Maria Cubau, Carmen Cusack, Claudia G. Flores, and Erin Weston, among others. Also, Zen buddies Chris Ives, Dan Leighton, and Dale Wright put in their two cents. They know I probably shoulda been a doctor.

Then there was the growl of that wild cat heard while hitchin' a ride all the way to Nashville . . .

Disclaimer: All narratives contained herein are exaggerated, distorted, or otherwise taken out of context. Read with caution, and enjoy.

This book, like that old missive to Kyushu, is for all the angel-headed hipsters out there. They know who they are.

Game Plan
Using Zen Principles to Overcome Obstacles and Achieve Your Career Goals

Mountains Are Mountains:
Roots of Everyday Stress

Introduction	Chapter One	Chapter Two
APPLYING ZEN	ZEN AND PROFESSIONAL LEADERSHIP	THE POWER OF ZEN
On making use of a Zen-based experience of intuitive insight, which is not a thought process but a state of existence	Introducing the relation between Zen and the business world, and why the workplace is in need of Zen	Applying the steadiness and flexibility of the Unmoving Mind to professional interpersonal relations

Mountains Are Not Mountains:
Transforming Conflict into Opportunity

Chapter Three	Chapter Four	Chapter Five
EVERYBODY MUST GET FOXED	THE GREATER THE DOUBT, THE GREATER THE ENLIGHTENMENT	SEEING THE FOREST, BUT NOT MISSING THE TREES
Why do obstacles block the path to professional development based on deficiencies in self-discipline?	Transforming feelings of hopelessness by experiencing the Great Doubt	Activating and integrating the Hermit's intuition and the Warrior's spontaneity

Mountains Are Mountains Again:
From Structure to Anti-Structure

Chapter Six	Chapter Seven	Chapter Eight
RETURNING TO THE MARKETPLACE	ALL'S WELL THAT ENDS WELL	COMING FROM NOWHERE TO SOMEWHERE
Advantages of Zen Encounters over Confrontations for ending conflict and achieving mutual productivity	Four Steps for dealing with problems in organizational structure through creative ways of speaking and silence	The immediacy and eccentricity of enacting anti-structural approaches

PART ONE

Mountains Are Mountains: Roots of Everyday Stress

Two monks were arguing. One said the flag was moving in the wind and the other said the wind was moving the flag. Along came the master who said, "It's not the flag moving or the wind moving. It's your mind."

Zen koan about the
Sixth Patriarch

Introduction: Applying Zen

A Book Not About, but From Zen

WHEN IN JAPAN, I am often asked about the purpose of my visit. The expected answer is that, like many other foreigners, I came to work in the Japanese corporate world. When I say that my purpose is to study Zen Buddhism, I am usually asked in a very perplexed way about why Americans are so interested in such an old fashioned tradition. A passenger on the bullet train once told me he never went to Buddhist temples because, "When you've seen one, you've seen them all."

On the other hand, an American friend currently working in Japan was told by her Japanese colleagues that if she wanted to understand the corporate structure she should learn something about Japanese religion, especially Zen. For example, they pointed out that since 1937 employees in every Matsushita (Panasonic) factory around the world begin their workday by reciting seven principles based on a kind of religious training that emphasizes the qualities of service, fairness, teamwork, improvement, humility, accepting change, and gratitude. Over time, I began to realize that my friend's colleagues were right: we cannot appreciate the dynamics of Japanese business practices without understanding the profound underlying connection with Zen. At the same time, I have come to feel that the workplace in America can also benefit from the spirituality of Zen to promote the discipline and self-control that contribute to mutually beneficial productivity.

This is not a book **about** Zen; it does not provide historical analysis or guidance in meditation or monastic ritual. I do not describe the formation of the institution or literature of the Zen Buddhist sect in East Asia; nor do I give instructions on how to meditate. There are many excellent scholarly works as well as notable popular books that do these things.

Instead, this book is **from** Zen. It adapts traditional ideals and styles of training to the goal of improving interpersonal relations in the professional sphere. It explains how to present yourself more effectively to the outside world by unifying your emotions and thoughts, cultivating a lucid, insightful, and powerful way of self-development and expression. I have spent many years of study and have a deep appreciation for the Zen Buddhist tradition. My aim here, however, is to apply some ideas derived from Zen principles and related teachings in a practical way to real situations that all of us encounter on a regular basis.

The aim is to **make use** of a Zen-based experience of intuitive insight, which is not a thought process but a state of existence. In the records of the classical masters, the Zen mind is expressed in seemingly eccentric, irreverent, or unconventional behavior. The heroes of these tales are known for slapping each other or performing other outrageous acts, such as leaping from poles or cutting off fingers, in flagrant disregard of strict monastic discipline. They did not break conventional social rules as an anarchic spiritual rebellion but, rather, to enhance and strengthen institutional **structure** by exercising a distinctive brand of creativity that I refer to as **anti-structure** (derived from anthropologist Victor Turner).

Zen can help with personal interactions as well as business relationships. However, **White Collar Zen** draws a clear distinction between the private world, which is based on the intimacy of an emotional exchange between individuals, and the professional realm, in which personal feelings must be set aside to avoid bias or favoritism in the pursuit of common workplace goals.

The benefit of White Collar Zen is that it helps deal with situations that challenge your position or status at work, like the cases of a promotion denied or delayed or an unwanted assignment. Instead of letting obstacles become a source of conflict or confrontation through petty, turf-hungry reactions, by maintaining clarity and focus you transform an impasse into a chance for development.

Can Zen insight really be applied to the humdrum activity of modern society? Does not a practical understanding of Zen Buddhism require meditating in a Japanese temple, trekking in remote mountains, or breathing the alpine air while refining an aesthetic appreciation of nature? There are indeed historical and cultural barriers to appropriating the philosophy rooted in medieval East Asian hermitic traditions. I contend, however, that inspiration can be garnered from Zen with neither formal study that follows the rules of monastic life nor reclusive wandering outside the ordinary social order. According to an old Chinese saying alluded to in Zen writings,

- *Small hermits conceal themselves in hills and thickets,*
  Great hermits conceal themselves in palaces and towns.

Zen insight highlights familiar spiritual tendencies that are already at least partially developed by all of us and can be attained in a variety of ways. In ordinary life, according to Zen, we tend to act and react in either a mechanical or chaotic manner governed by instincts and reflexes, and then try to overcome inappropriate feelings arising from attachments or partiality of perspective by the application of logic. We attempt to be "objective." However, when reason is unable to resolve crises in interpersonal relations, it is necessary to step back and experience a sense of quietude beyond the drone of ordinary life.

The Zen practice of zazen (sitting meditation) leads to a state of calm composure whether performed at home or at a Buddhist center with a *samgha* (assembly of practitioners). The aim is to learn to hear the inner voice that draws us to a deeper, more inclusive sense of perception and understanding. Another Zen technique is to contemplate paradoxical or absurd **koans** (quixotic utterance or pedagogical riddle), such as "What is the sound of one hand clapping?" or "Does a dog have Buddha-nature (or innate quality of enlightenment)?"

Many people have found their own methods for accessing the inner voice not necessarily associated with a particular tradition. This may involve withdrawing from the cacophony of worldly affairs and quieting the spirit in solitude, away from the crowd, or listening to music, going for walks, or spending the day in the woods or at the beach. For others quietude is attained through an activity or discipline such as running, exercise, playing a sport, practicing an art form or music, or training in yoga. Participating in community service or ritual conduct are other ways of helping to cast aside the cares of everyday existence that get in the way of spiritual reflection. A scholar of contemporary religions has pointed out that the decline in America's organized mainstream ritual practice does not necessarily indicate a waning of spirituality:

- *People today say they can find God sitting on the beach, at night, under the sky, in their relationships, or their service work.*

Doing zazen or studying koans in addition to the sorts of activities mentioned above can be understood as useful tools or means to the end of turning on the interior light switch, rather than as goals in themselves. Just as useful are shamanistic vision quest techniques such as sensory deprivation or walking about in the wilderness, also a favorite activity of classical Zen masters.

However, the essence of Zen is not a particular style of practice but **a way of being** based on understanding the nature of the inner self in relation to outer reality. Unlike most styles of spirituality, Zen does not look for truth beyond the human realm. In offering a concentrated and comprehensive approach to developing the power of **Intuition**, it shows the importance of self-control in all aspects of existence.

Zen promotes experiences of clarity that usually pass us by in the muddled busyness of our daily lives. It highlights the twofold nature of reality. Nothing is black or white. Victories are snatched from the jaws of defeat and vice versa. We have defeats that teach lessons as well as triumphs that need to be sustained, all conditioned by our ability or inability to adjust to the shifting tide. In Zen sayings, monks who convince themselves they are on the verge of a breakthrough are "nothing but wild fox spirits," and those who at one point seem utterly defeated are "ones who come back to life in the midst of death."

Finding Your Own Zen

During a visit to the magnificent shrine at Nikko, located deep in the mountains north of Tokyo, I was walking up from the station to the main hall and stopped by the "sacred bridge" (*shinkyo*) that crosses a rushing stream. The cascading sound of the water overwhelmed any distraction. At first, it drowned out every other physical or mental phenomenon that might be "heard." The silence made its own kind of deafening roar. It spontaneously led to a state of contemplation that allowed me to concentrate on several issues I was considering. I thought of the Zen saying,

- *The sounds of the valley streams are the Buddha's tongue,*
  The colors of the leaves on the mountains are his body.

After sitting for a while, I found I could control the level and transform the sound of the water through the power of the mind, turning it up or down as if with the dial of a radio. This experience, which began with a raw, immediate sensation, taught me an important lesson in the ability to exercise self-discipline.

Reflecting on the experience, I realized how Zen-like it was, and also that Zen is something evolving and deeply personal. Even in its classical period, Zen Buddhism was not a single, simple ideology or a pure, pristine, autonomous religious institution but was inextricably wedded to its cultural context. Zen is a complex historical phenomenon, part and parcel of various religious and social trends, absorbing and assimilating a myriad of influences. Today, Zen remains a syncretistic amalgamation that combines and intertwines various elements developed over the centuries. Zen is Zen in that it has a distinctive flavor and style, yet Zen is also not Zen in that it is diverse and diffused.

Think of a computer-imaging file that is transferred from system to system. Each time it is moved, it looks a bit blurrier around the edges. This is like the history of Zen, first spreading in East Asian countries and now splashing onto the shores of America. However, the blurriness should not be understood as a decline in quality. In the process of transmission, much is gained and strengthened, like the ability to enhance and manipulate the file. The movement that may appear to be a decline is actually a renewal.

Zen started coming to America at the end of the nineteenth century. It has not been transmitted as a uniform entity with a single essence, but has arrived in a fragmented, specialized, and idiosyncratic manner. For many, Zen functions as an ethnic religion of Japanese immigrant communities, especially in Hawaii, California, and Brazil. As in Japan, one of the main roles of the Zen institution for these communities is the provision of a funerary rite for commemorating dead ancestors during mortuary ceremonies, memorial services, and the annual Obon or Ghost Festival. But the traditional institutional structures of Zen in Japan have not been carried over without undergoing significant change. As ethnic communities got increasingly assimilated into American society, the pattern of ritual life was refashioned.

Zen has also been transmitted as an "alternative altar" for Americans seeking solace in mystical spirituality outside the

Judeo-Christian mainstream. There are now dozens of thriving Zen centers, some founded by monks from China, Japan, Korea, or Vietnam, and others by Western seekers who have studied or traveled extensively in pursuit of an authentic heritage or lineage. New centers are located in both urban and rural areas, not only on the West Coast but throughout the country. No matter how much they may follow a traditional model, their styles of practice are conditioned by Western cultural attitudes, especially concerning gender roles, individual rights, and environmental and technology issues.

There is also another broader component of American Zen. Many intellectuals and mystics, who have been influenced by diverse trends in psychotherapy, literature, New Age spirituality and healing, have sought to achieve peace of mind by using Zen techniques. The Zen promise of realization through enhanced self-awareness has become an object of fascination and longing.

Particularly intriguing is the way Zen in traditional China and Japan developed a rich variety of art forms. These range from the literary and fine arts (poetry, painting, calligraphy) to the martial arts (karate, sword fighting, and archery) and the practical arts (gardening, flower arranging, and tea ceremony). Artistic skill is an accomplishment attained in the present moment, unaffected by attachment to people or things, not an egoistic pursuit of recognition for its own sake.

Another important factor in the transmission of Zen to America are the tactics and strategies expressed in *The Book of Five Rings* by the invincible sword master Miyamoto Musashi. These works have been appropriated by the worlds of business and management and used as textbooks for operating contemporary commercial affairs.

The Zen approach to discipline has been distilled in books like *Zen and the Art of Motorcycle Maintenance* by Robert Pirsig, which is a send-up of the original *Zen in the Art of Archery* by Eugen Herrigel and its countless imitators. Pirsig's work uses the image

of the motorcycle as a symbol of interior development. It opens
with the epigram,

- *The real cycle you're working on is a cycle called "yourself."*

The parts of the motorcycle are dispensable and replaceable but
the intuitive dimension of the inner self, which Zen refers to as the
Unmoving Mind, remains unperturbed in spite of constant shifts
and changes.

The image of the motorcycle also calls to mind the way in which
Zen has been associated and disseminated through Japanese pop
culture, such as Manga (comics) and Martial Arts. These cultural
phenomena, along with the steady stream of books such as *The
Zen of Oz*, *Tao-Jones*, and *The Tao of Pooh*, have helped Zen infil-
trate the common consciousness.

Therefore, there are many possibilities for you to discover
your own way of appropriating Buddhism or of "being Zen." I
remember planning for my first trip to spend a year doing research in Japan. I had heard so many different comments that
were contradictory—Tokyo is the most exciting city on earth or
Tokyo is overcrowded and ugly; the Japanese people are open and
sincere or the Japanese will never trust foreigners. I asked my Japanese teacher what to expect. She said,

- *Expect to find your own Japan.*

Recently my son, taking an advanced writing class in middle
school, was required practically every day to compose a different
style of poem that reflected his personal experiences or attitudes.
At the end of the report period he was to collect several dozen
poems he had written and organize them into a book. My wife
pointed out that one poem said that he was talkative and outgo-
ing, but another one written a few weeks later mentioned something about being shy and withdrawn. She asked what would
happen if this contradiction was noticed. I advised my son that
in that case he should speak up and say to the teacher,

- *Hey, don't box me in.*

This same advice applies to Zen in the workplace. What it can offer will vary by person and circumstance. Zen has a history of proposing insights and attitudes that can sound downright contradictory yet are sensible and compelling when applied to concrete human experience. As you read this book and think about your own professional life, do not be locked into any assumption. Finding your own brand of Zen is a matter of internal development that can help you take control by overcoming stress, making the most of disappointment, and conquering disillusioning situations created by external factors. According to a Zen saying, it is time to,

- *Grab the tiger by the whiskers.*

CHAPTER ONE

Zen and Professional Leadership

Japanese Business and Social Values

EVERYONE IN THE WORKPLACE these days is looking for ways to create opportunities for advancement and growth while minimizing the conditions that produce the irritability and lack of productivity that characterize burnout. The times are fast fading when a domineering boss can relate to employees by making tyrannical demands or act out as an autocrat who rules with an iron fist and orders people around without any attempt to enlist their cooperation. According to an article on "Monster Managers" in *American Way*,

- *We all know them. Some of us have even worked for them. But like the dinosaur, their days are numbered.*

Managers today are expected to be leaders and to motivate and inspire by creating a cohesive atmosphere for the sake of achieving common aims. A successful leader fosters teamwork to support individual creativity and forge alliances. *The Economist* recently ran an ad seeking an executive, who would fit the following description,

- *With great communication, negotiation and influencing skills, you command respect and credibility and build effective partnerships, motivating staff and promoting inclusiveness.*

However, the hierarchical structure of professional and business organizations ensures that the contests experienced on a daily basis tend to thwart collaborative efforts and lead to tension and conflict. Therefore, many professionals are now turning to alternative sources of values in order to alleviate the causes of strife, while honing talents that keep them competitive. "Soul Providers," another article in *American Way* states,

- *A growing number of companies tend to the spirits of their workers—and watch their employees blossom.*

According to the author's survey, 80 percent of CEOs "intended to utilize their spiritual values in all future strategies."

White-collar managers and employees alike are investigating various forms of mysticism, ranging from Kabbala and Quakerism to Yoga and Zen Buddhism, and reading books like *Jesus, CEO* and *What Would Buddha Do at Work?* Spirituality provides a common, uplifting perspective that offers peace and clarity of mind. The *Miami Herald* reported, "From Torah to yoga classes, professionals make time for quiet contemplation," and cited numerous cases of people feeling sharper and more relaxed as a result. One participant in meditation, an accountant, commented,

- *I center myself. It helps me achieve a balance within.*

White Collar Zen incorporates traditional Zen techniques that can help you become persuasive and effective in handling everyday affairs of the business world. Great masters from the golden age of Zen in China and Japan (especially the ninth through thirteenth centuries) perfected techniques for transformative self-awareness in attaining the Unmoving Mind, which is characterized by steadiness and firm conviction accompanied by flexibility and the ability to maneuver through difficult circumstances. To cultivate this

state on a permanent basis, Zen masters set up monastic training systems that were as serious and rigorous as any forms of discipline in the history of civilization.

But these highly disciplined masters could also be eccentric and irreverent to a degree verging on blasphemy. They displayed as keen a sense of irony and absurdity as you will ever find. Their words and actions expressed ecstatic freedom, breaking the grip of all conventional forms of structure. A creative approach to professional interpersonal relations can preserve that incredibly productive tension between the elements of discipline or structure and the opposing forces of irreverence or anti-structure.

Some of the recent interest in Zen Buddhism has been sparked by a larger fascination with Japanese social values, which have been a source of inspiration for business leaders seeking ways to maximize efficiency and teamwork. However, admiration for Japanese values and their impact on business practices, understandably, has waxed and waned with the vicissitudes of the marketplace.

During the East Asian economic "miracle" of the 1970s and 1980s, featuring Japan as the Great Tiger (or Dragon) along with the Four Cubs (S. Korea, Taiwan, Hong Kong, Singapore), corporate America sought to learn as much as possible, both from and about, the secrets of the successes of the leading trade partner of the global economy, Japan Inc. The bestseller lists featured books like *Japan is Number One, A Guide for Westerners to the Mind of Modern Japan*, and *The Four Little Dragons*.

Efforts to import the **Kaizen** methodology of quality control and continuous improvement techniques spawned a publication boom. Japanese business, it was said, mastered long-term planning and guaranteed customer satisfaction through a standardized system of teamwork management and shared responsibilities. A typical evaluation was,

- *Japanese companies are thinking a quarter century ahead while American companies are thinking only of the next quarter.*

A corollary assumption was that the economic boom rested on exceptionally worthwhile social values. The economic boom reflected a unique convergence of traditional spirituality and contemporary methods of production. Religious principles derived from Confucian and Zen Buddhist practices of self-sacrificing loyalty and unstinting commitment to disciplined activity were thought to represent an enhanced Eastern version of the shopworn Protestant work ethic that was highly adaptable to the modern workplace. According to a Japanese executive, who during the bubble economy headed Mitsukoshi, the largest department store in Japan,

- *We succeed because we combine the pragmatic management techniques of the West with the spiritual, intuitive aspects of the East.*

If there was any uneasiness in those years, it was because Japan seemed to be assuming an overly dominant and almost defiant role in the global marketplace. Americans feared that the once-defeated military enemy was actually winning the new economic war. "From Pearl Harbor to Wall Street" was a saying of the day, along with images of the Statue of Liberty wearing a kimono and Japan-bashing ditties like, "If your children sneeze and the dog has fleas, blame it on the Japanese."

Movies from the 1980s and 1990s at once revered and reviled the Japanese ethic. Among them were *Gung Ho!*, which depicted a Japanese company taking over a failed auto plant in the United States; *Black Rain*, a film about Yakuza (Japanese mob) control of economic forces, *Rising Sun*, which hinted at multinational corporate conspiracies based on Japanese superiority; and *Mr. Baseball*, chronicling the weaknesses of an American sports star in adjusting to the rigorous lifestyle in Japan.

With the bursting of the economic bubble, especially since the 1997 market crash, Japan now seems so diminished that it can be referred to as a "beleaguered backwater." The new trend is to deconstruct the Japanese corporate world. Numerous books focus on the cause of Japan's economic doldrums. Some highlight the deficiencies of **Kaisha**, or the Japanese corporate structure, exposing how its fundamental inflexibility results in stagnation, cronyism, and inefficiency rather than dynamic change and growth. At one time, Japanese companies were credited with incredible long-term planning. Now it is said that these companies, protected by state-run policies favoring the monopolistic trends that characterized pre-war *zaibatsu* (conglomerates), have pursued a shortsighted policy of bad loans and investments. Under titles such as *Lost Japan, The System that Soured*, and *Demystifying*

Japan, the culture of herd mentality and blind obedience to the *iemoto* (company patriarch) has become a model for how your company should not behave.

The Warrior and the Hermit

Does this changed perception mean that Japanese social values are now suddenly irrelevant to American business, or are there principles that continue to be inspirational and useful? On the level of popular culture, the enduring appeal of the "3 N's" of Ninjas, Nintendo, and aNime (animation) testifies to a continued appreciation of traditional Japanese folklore about the exploits of saints and warriors interacting with ghosts, ghouls, and demons innovatively presented with the latest hi-tech special effects.

Many people are looking beyond the ups and downs of the economy to learn lessons from the apparently timeless wisdom of Asian mystical thought. Zen combines some of the best elements of two ideal, yet seemingly contradictory, forms of behavior in medieval Japan, the **Warrior** and the **Hermit**, which can be effectively applied to contemporary affairs.

The Art of War, an ancient Chinese text, and the Japanese work, *The Book of Five Rings*, have been required reading in business (as well as military) schools for many years. "Striking Where They Least Expect It" and "Moving Swiftly to Overcome Your Competitors" are two of the six principles recommended for managers in Mark McNeilly's *Sun Tzu and the Art of Business*. In *The Art of the Advantage*, Kaihan Krippendorff suggests that in some of the major battles between Coca Cola and Pepsi or WalMart versus Sears or Kirin versus Asahi beer, the companies that prevailed owed their success to their application, for the most part unwitting, of some of the basic **Art of War** strategies.

Art of War teachings help a corporation seize advantage of an adversary's inability to adjust to changing conditions. In open battle between corporations, the methods of medieval Japanese warriors can instill strategies based on such principles as "luring the tiger from the hills." Methods used to create ambush situations by means of decoys and disguises that disarm and defeat the rival provide a readily available template for strategizing. These techniques are designed to mask one's own weaknesses and minimize losses while relentlessly exposing and attacking the areas of vulnerability in the opponent.

For example, if your company's main rival is known for its distribution in a downtown market, then it is necessary to lure them to compete in your suburban stronghold and watch as they overextend their resources and verge on collapse. Staying wedded to a specific strategy may prove ineffective with another rival, and it will be necessary to shift as soon as your competitor compensates. A hallmark of Art of War is this open-ended understanding of multiple options, avoiding the trap of being locked or fixed on any particular outlook that may quickly become obsolete or produce diminishing returns.

The ruthless, manipulative, winner-takes-all strategies of the Art of War, with its use of deception, deviousness, and duplicity, are suited to contests between companies. This paradigm works well when victory is the goal, as in the saying evoked in both the book and film versions of *Rising Sun*,

- *Business is war.*

But when dealing with colleagues and peers within the company, with whom it is important to cooperate and share the glory, Art of War must be modified and complemented with the ideals and methods of the Hermit way for achieving a calm composure through a withdrawal and renunciation of petty conflicts. The Hermit is the archetype of dedication to principles and wholehearted commitment to idealism.

In integrating the Warrior and Hermit approaches, Zen Buddhist training provides a timely new paradigm for being clear in thoughts and disciplined in actions to establish harmonious interpersonal relations and attain mutually beneficial goals. The intracorporate world is competitive, as people vie for promotions, raises, bonuses, and resources in an environment that is limited and constrained. The pie can be cut into just so many pieces and money cannot be printed. To succeed in this realm, it is necessary to develop Kaizen or quality control methods for insuring customer satisfaction while reducing the excesses of an unreconstructed Kaisha or inflexible approach through traditional techniques for cultivating contemplation and concentration.

Like Art of War discourse, White Collar Zen features flexibility and agility in keeping others guessing while not getting caught off guard yourself, as well as the ability to adjust to shifting circumstances. It seeks to weed out flaws and make the most of limitations in one's own situation, while transforming impasses and obstacles into progressive opportunities. Some observers argue that this facility is enabling Japan Inc. to reform its global outreach and recover from times of economic hardship.

This approach is expressed in the martial arts saying that all your energy can be summoned in a decisive moment:

- *Put a lifetime of effort into a single shot of the bow.*

Doing this can only be achieved by evoking the Hermit way to release from a partial outlook based on intuition beyond ordinary thinking.

The aim is to be spontaneous yet decisive and strategic in handling crises by acting and reacting fully in the here and now, without the hesitation that lets opportunities slip away. Compared to many avenues to self-growth that rely on an otherworldly source of truth, Zen develops the potential for practical accomplishments possessed by each person but perhaps not yet realized. It develops the skill of thoughtful yet compelling speaking as well as silence—using both words and no-words—to communicate persuasively with those who might otherwise prove uncooperative in order to bring about positive change in everyday interactions.

Art of War suggests how to manipulate through delay and de-
terrence and by heightening conflict, whereas White Collar Zen's
simplicity and harmony work to overcome challenges and achieve
common goals. This expands the size of the pie or distributes it
equitably for the advantage of all co-workers, replacing the Art of
War saying, "Know yourself and know your enemy, and win 100
battles," with,

- *Know yourself and know your colleagues, and accomplish*
  100 goals together.

The Unmoving Mind—and How to Get It

The Unmoving Mind is characterized by a firmness and lack of
vacillation that derives from confidence and inner strength. In
the face of disruption, the Mind remains sure and stable, undis-
turbed by distractions and obstructions. Founded on an inalter-
able certitude, it remains steady in the midst of constant change.
Facing high stakes and great doubts, there is no force that can
budge its commitment to principles.

However, the Unmoving Mind is by no means rigid. The Mind
is reflective and neutral. It adapts the reclusive, transcendental
path of the Hermit that roots out the weeds of bias by removing
personal interest or gain. The Hermit, or solitary artist, ascetic,
or pilgrim who renounces worldly attachments in search of spiritual truth, is willing to give up all pursuits based on desire and
attachment. Standing back and detached from emotions, he looks
objectively at the world from a thoroughly impartial standpoint.

At the same time, the Zen Mind is alert and responsive, subdu-
ing and resolving conflicts with the fearlessness of the active path
of the Warrior or samurai. As celebrated in countless legends, the
Warrior followed the Bushido code of honor, relinquishing his
own interests out of fierce loyalty to a higher authority. If his
master was killed, the **Ronin**, leaderless samurai, literally a "wave

person" floating aimlessly outside of any structure) lived only to avenge his death and then commit suicide. The Warrior's tough-minded strategies are based on the assumptions:

- *The weak are meat, the strong eat;* and
  The nail that stands up gets hammered into place.

Strict discipline must be enforced.

The Warrior ideal, which is group oriented and results based, seems at odds with the Hermit, who strives for uninvolved detachment and communion with nature. Yet both approaches emphasize dedication and self-reliance and are committed to giving up personal interest for a broader realm of benefits. White Collar Zen seeks to synthesize the Warrior, who remains committed to enacting change and swoops down into productive negotiation in the valley of everyday affairs, with the Hermit, who stands beyond worldly turmoil by dwelling on the peak. Both archetypes, one appearing active and the other inactive, share a determination and perseverance to complete a mission, leaving no stone unturned. No obstacle is too great, no sacrifice too severe. The Unmoving Mind does not remain detached and aloof, but is eminently active in concrete affairs in exerting a sense of authority that breaks down barriers to resolve impasses constructively.

A typically ironic, double-edged Zen saying addresses the issue of stress by asking rhetorically,

- *What's the fuss? Every day is a good day!*

This might be taken as a naive affirmation of the status quo, seeing no need for spiritual development, restructuring of priorities, or techniques for enhancement. But it really means that each day can be made good through your capacity for self-control. You learn to gaze beyond the world of ordinary trials and tribulations beyond joy and sorrow, optimism and pessimism, and other artificial oppositions.

The Zen Mind or Unmoving Mind contributes to the successful professional's leadership skills by at once sharpening the ability to negotiate the intricacies of the channels of hierarchy and stimulating charisma or free-flowing creativity that is unbounded by rules and protocol. The professional administrator, like the Zen master, knows when to disclose or to withhold while weighing the relative strengths of proposals in an imperfect world. Both kinds of leaders have a knack for handling the details of projects and personnel in a careful yet forceful fashion, whether using soft/tender or harsh/tough methods of training. Seeing an employee or trainee overworked and underpaid, they can rectify this with a soothing and indulgent approach as expressed in the Zen saying,

- *Do whatever it takes to stop the baby from crying.*

But, they can also evaluate a colleague or subordinate swiftly and effectively if that is what it takes to create far-reaching remedies. According to another typical epigram,

- *You have to be cruel to be kind.*

I had a senior colleague who was an inspiring mentor for many different kinds of students and junior colleagues, a role called **Senpai** in Japanese (the same "sen," meaning former, as in Sensei or teacher). Senpai always went out of his way to lend a helping hand. He had several prized pupils on whom he lavished praise and opened doors. As a result, we were stunned to hear of his brusque treatment of a brilliant disciple, who had left his tutelage and moved on to another position. Senpai was proud of his disciple's accomplishments. When she called the first time for advice, he was happy to accommodate. But when she called him a second time in the midst of a crisis, he told her he did not have time for her and hung up the phone.

Her initial reaction was that he was abandoning her because he could not handle the fact that she was making it on her own. It took the disciple several months to get over the hurt. When she later realized that his aim had been to force her to reach a higher degree of self-reliance, she eventually was able to look back and appreciate what at the time had seemed like nothing other than a slap in the face. From this new vantage point, she understood that underneath the gruff exterior there was a kind, gentle touch on Senpai's part. He had not at all turned his back on her. She made a point of shaking his hand when she saw him some time after. This lesson resonates with the Confucian admonition,

- *If I show you one corner of the room, I do not want to have to show you the other three.*

So saith Confucius, CEO.

According to traditional Zen teaching the imperturbable Mind cannot be swayed, no matter the temptation. Thirteenth-century master **Dogen**, founder of Soto Zen, one of the two main Zen sects in Japan, was traveling from his secluded monastery in the remote mountains of northern Japan to the new capital city in Kamakura. The capital had been in Kyoto for centuries (and would soon be moved back). But a new shogun (generalisimo) wanted to establish his base of power in the east, and was eager to build temples in Kamakura on a grand scale modeled after China.

Intrigued by the recent rapid growth of the Zen sect, the shogun summoned Dogen, and offered to make him abbot of one of the impressive new temples, Kenchoji, which still stands today. Disillusioned by the corruption and worldliness of the shogun's approach to Zen, Dogen unceremoniously declined the offer and returned to his mountain retreat and a life dedicated to religious training. He penned the following verse,

- *Moonlight framing*
  A small boat
  Drifting in the sea—
  Tossed not by the waves
  Nor swayed by the breeze.

Soon after this episode, Dogen heard that one of his disciples had said he would consider accepting the shogun's offer. Dogen had the disciple expelled from the temple. His seat was dug up and thrown away, and no one else was ever allowed to occupy that spot. Dogen, CEO, integrated the Hermit's loftiness and transcendence of ordinary procedures with the Warrior's daring and dedication. He eliminated Kaisha-like deficiencies in his monastic system and showed how to maintain Kaizen-based quality control, beginning by rejecting corrupted relations and overcoming conflicts in organizational structure.

CHAPTER TWO

The Power of Zen

Power Used, Abused, and So Misused

P ROFESSIONAL RELATIONS as part of a hierarchical structure reflect a struggle for power. Contest and competitions are
useful and necessary to test and cultivate abilities. In deliberations and negotiations, you may want to seize control. You have
to tread carefully, however, because the toes you step on today
may be connected to the feet you will have to worship tomorrow.
How can you achieve power that becomes part of your character
rather than something that can be taken away or lost? White Collar Zen seeks to clarify the notion,

- *Power, use it or lose it—but don't abuse it.*

In the popular TV series *Dallas*, Jock Ewing usually left control of the family oil business in the hands of the cold-blooded,
Machiavellian son, J. R., a character all America loved to hate. J. R.
explained his recipe for success: "The first step is to give up integrity. After that, it's a piece of cake." In one episode, J. R. got in hot
water and Jock handed over the reins to the idealistic son Bobby.
Not used to having power, Bobby quickly managed to overstep

his bounds and he was called on the carpet. When Bobby defended himself on the grounds that he'd been given the power to make decisions, Jock grabbed him by the collar and said,

- *I gave you the power? Then you ain't got nothin', boy. Power's not something you're given. It's something you take.*

In Zen, however, power is neither given nor taken. Nor does it represent the accumulation of assets. Power is not a matter of adding up years of experience, education credentials, rank or status. It should not be captured by intimidation. Real and enduring power comes through strength of character and genuine self-confidence stemming from an unpremeditated display of dignity and eagerness to accept responsibility.

The less you demand power, because you have risen above the concerns of ego, the more you command the respect and admiration of colleagues, who recognize the impact of your words and deeds. The more you transcend the mundane world, the more effectively you are able to operate within it. The hidden spiritual side, like the roots of a tree that are concealed from view, is essential for the trunks and branches of professional life to thrive. Rather than holding sway over others, obstacles are overcome and momentum built through the mutual benefits of constructive interpersonal engagement.

White Collar Zen attains power by cultivating the inner self and its sense of mastery over the flow of events to foster cooperation and positive change. In Japan, instead of saying, "Good luck," people tell each other, "Work hard!" implying that opportunities are created from within. However, true power in Zen is not derived from your accomplishments alone. You must look beyond your own vantage point to take in the greater well-being of the community. Neither defeat nor victory is seen as personal, so failure and success alike can be taken in stride.

An organization is a vehicle for creative expression, which can bring goals to fruition. Entering into an organizational structure is invigorating because it provides avenues of command that enable you to create and fulfill a vision. But all too often, the structure presents a labyrinthine path leading only to frustration. It fosters a Kafkaesque feeling of helplessness by generating expectations that cannot be met, given limitations in resources or obstructions that often seem senseless.

When a problem arises in your bailiwick that seems to be caused by inefficiency or confusion in the system, further impediments are often thrown in your path by the bureaucratic structure, which seems hellbent to frustrate attempts to find a remedy. This is the Catch-22 of the professional sphere. Once disturbed, the machinery of red tape and triplicate forms appears determined, as if it had a mind of its own, to preserve the status quo. It gives no support or solace to those who might disturb its inertia, even—or especially—when their aim is correction and reform. This kind of inflexibility and resistance to change is thought to be part of the reason for the downfall of the Japanese corporate system, but it is found in every organization.

The very structure that represents freedom invariably becomes a source of constraint, even a kind of prison. You seek to travel a path toward greater accomplishments and rewards and end up trudging along to and from the dungeon of despair. Procedures, routines, and rules of etiquette and protocol can be daunting for the novice. Hierarchy based on credentials, background, experience, service, seniority, salary, rank, and connections blocks upward mobility. Casting about for solutions, you know that the clock is ticking and that you will be the one held responsible for any failure or decline in productivity, or loss of prestige and momentum. Reacting from emotion means that you may be doomed to alienate possible supporters and create a vicious cycle of disillusion and defeat. Yet logic alone does not provide effective solutions.

Senpai had a friend who was named supervisor of a special account in a financial management firm. This was a substantial promotion she had been seeking for a long time, with a new title, office space, personnel, and additional perks and resources. She felt that she had been elevated to **Daimyo** status, in that she was now a kind of midlevel samurai overseeing underlings though still subservient to the supreme commander or Shogun. She soon learned, however, that the account was fashioned by earmarks and claims, contingencies and hidden subdivisions, and held the potential for considerable shortfall. Moreover, she found herself under pressure from various colleagues, who sought more consultation before she made commitments on certain segments of the account that affected the overall budget.

Shortly after taking over, her "Ronin complex" began to kick in. Looking at the computer screen one fine morning, she realized the budget was minus X thousands of dollars that were there the day before. Several initiatives might have to be delayed or terminated, even though the funds existed in principle. Or did they? Was this a clerical or accounting error that could be easily corrected, or evidence of significant miscommunication or disagreement? Had she been misled as to the extent of her authority? When she inquired, she received no clear answer. The accountants could only tell her what was in or not in the budget. Others consulted indicated that the jurisdiction was in fact hers. A round of inquiries went nowhere fast. Feeling powerless, she wondered about the intentions of those who seemed to stand in her path and obstruct a resolution. Promoted to a spot at the heart of the organization, she nonetheless felt that she had been cut off from or abandoned by the very structure that was sustaining her.

To explain human motives Zen draws on traditional Chinese and Japanese folk tales. The causes of frustration and failure are illustrated with fables about magical shape-shifting foxes. In Asia, the mythical **Fox** is the primary symbol of how you can become entangled in a web of misunderstanding. The Fox, which appears to its unwitting victim in human form, represents the miasma of deception and duplicity that brings with it self-doubt and frustrates the pursuit of aspirations. It generally comes to someone who is vulnerable because of a flaw of character, such as a wayward mate, errant priest or disloyal warrior, all of whom betray a code of honorable behavior. The Fox is a symbol of undesirable tendencies, such as chasing after unattainable aims while leaving important parts of life unattended.

Along with Foxes who deceive, however, there are always **Buddhas** who are eager to support, not because of personal ties or loyalty, but because they objectively evaluate the merits and demerits of a situation. Yet Buddhas may remain obscure and unrecognized. Both the Fox and the Buddha are often disguised and each tries to pass as the other for strategic purposes. Distinguishing between them is a valuable skill. As decisions hang in the balance, the Unmoving Mind is a tool to separate truth or authenticity from illusion or untruth. Illusion renders you vulnerable to anxiety and confusion and unable to react to critical situations with clarity and lucidity.

What is unique about folklore in East Asia is that good and evil are always intertwined so that it is important to see one side manifested in the midst of the reverse tendency. The Fox's functions need not be entirely negative. The experience of illusion can also have a positive side, representing a challenge that can inspire. Learning to unlearn bad habits is essential for success. When the Fox is transformed from a sign of inner weakness or vulnerability, the Buddha emerges as a positive image that represents the restoration of character through the discovery of strengths.

In contrast to what is portrayed in typical myth and legend, the Zen standpoint is that external factors are not really outside of you but are to be considered a reflection of interior levels of understanding, whether delusory or enlightened. Since all people harbor the potential to display the Fox-side or the Buddha-side of their innermost nature, these images in the exterior world are inseparable from inner character.

Dark Night of the Soul

My friend's doubt about whether she was foxed in managing the complex account could be debilitating if it caused her to hesitate and lose the chance to regain power. Doubt generally inhibits your ability to act-react spontaneously. An instant of uncertainty, for example, causes an athlete to miss a chance to score or a performer to lose an opportunity to demonstrate great mastery.

But doubt need not be just a source of nervous anxiety. Rather, it can lead to a profound reflection that serves to elevate self-understanding. An experience that is instrumental in spiritual attainment is known in Zen as the **Great Doubt**, which examines in a thoroughgoing way all assumptions and presuppositions. This resembles what medieval Christian mystics called the "Dark Night of the Soul," through which you must pass from the dark abyss of ignorance and self-deception to the heights and bright light of genuine insight. The Great Doubt takes nothing for granted and questions every outlook, and when applied to personal development it helps you act-react fully within—rather than half a step behind—this present moment. In contrast, unproductive doubt is preoccupied with second-guessing and revels in uncertainty.

An Unmoving Mind is expert at turning proverbial swords into the plowshares of cooperation and harmony. When you do not favor your own position but develop useful trade-offs and constructive compromises, the result is that you feel in control of timing and placement. Through yielding and nonaggression, you can gain acceptance for your agenda and priorities as well as articulate schedule and resource needs.

According to the Zen tradition even the most sacred and revered objects are mere conventions that can be treated with blasphemy and contempt. A famous saying of master **Lin-chi** (Rinzai in Japanese, founder of the Rinzai Zen sect) highlights the need to strip away the veneer of conventionality,

- *If you see the Buddha on the road, kill the Buddha!*

Lin-chi insists on transcending assumptions and attachments, even those concerning the ultimate model of enlightenment.

The importance of overcoming attachment is highlighted somewhat ironically by evoking the flip side of this enlightenment, a kind of sudden nonrealization, as expressed in a typically absurd Zen Buddhist koan. A monk is pushing an ox through a window. He is able to get the head, body, and legs through the opening, but the tail does not pass. Paradoxically, the large parts that logically ought not to fit are able to make it, but the one part that should go through easily cannot.

This recalls the biblical parable that it is easier to thread a camel through the eye of a needle than for a rich person to enter the Kingdom of God. The tail symbolizes ego, ignorance, or grasping, which at the eleventh hour prevents you from realizing your aims. Just one single element of obstruction manifested in a tiny instant of time is enough to block all the progress that has been made. A breakthrough must be accomplished with 100 percent effort and skill. Any slight obstacle can leave you hopelessly frustrated.

The process of **Elevation-Purification-Activation (EPA)** cultivates **four basic levels of human consciousness:** feeling or emotion, speaking or communication, thinking or logic, and knowing or intuitive awareness. According to this approach, if you allow yourself to be controlled by emotions, unchecked by introspection, inappropriate speech is the likely result. Feeling unsettled, disturbed, panicky, or anxious may cause you to say the wrong thing to the wrong person at the wrong time. The remedy is to elevate and purify personal feelings. When you attain the Hermit's objective, impersonal standpoint, you can articulate a higher vision that is effective in bringing about constructive change. Your emotions are tamed and transmuted into the foundation of a productive and cooperative understanding, which enables you to act with the Warrior's effortless creativity.

The goal of EPA is to resolve conflict and tension by means of a Zen **Encounter.** The Encounter reveals that power comes from the understanding that all parties benefit from a steady focus on productivity and good will. To avoid a **Confrontation** in the workplace, which heightens conflict and often ends in a no-win situation or dismay for at least one of the parties, the Encounter uses thought and speech in a constructive and cooperative way to achieve an opportunity for mutually enhancing dialogue and exchange of ideas. The Encounter is based on the ingenuity and calm composure of the Unmoving Mind. The Mind exhibits an aloof and unbiased perspective aligned with principles of fairness, reasonableness, and impartiality gained through contemplative insight and integrated with creative energy.

To create a deep sense of reconciliation and resolution through an Encounter, one must recognize and come to terms with the roots of conflict by identifying the cause of blockage without fearing the result of the inquiry or the possibilities of rejection. Suppose you are waiting to hear news of an expected raise, bonus, promotion, contract, or some other kind of award or reward for productive activities. Anticipating a payoff for hard work and a job well done, you learn that there are delays and uncertainties as to whether you will receive the benefit. To overcome the impasse, it is necessary to understand the gap between what you deserve and what you receive, or between some unattainable ideal and actual conditions. Keep expectations realistic and reasonable and methods flexible and fair in carrying out negotiations.

For Zen, the internal dimension is decisive in defining your degree of insight and accomplishment. The aim of the Encounter modality is to develop constantly the interior level through interaction with an exterior element. You cannot rest on your laurels or be satisfied until you test and contest your abilities through interaction with colleagues and counterparts. When I was a kid and heard that my father, a doctor, had a "practice," I wondered why he needed to keep practicing since he had already earned his credentials. Later, I came to understand that experts and professionals of all sorts need to make continuous progress in training in order to refine their skills. Each new situation is a test that determines who holds genuine power. No person is an island, and truth is determined only through a process of polishing your skills in order to foster mutual development. When you look out for the general good, enhancement invariably comes back to you as initiator.

There are **Four Steps** to complete a Zen Encounter, which will be explained in detail in the last two chapters. The steps are not a sequence to be memorized and blindly followed, but represent a flexible guideline that allows for creative movement from speech to silence and from structure to anti-structure, and back (and forth).

The process begins when you are able to distinguish and recognize a legitimate crisis in current structure. The steps continue with a creative approach to speaking (Step Two) as well as the use of silence when words fall short of the mark (Step Three). The guiding question for the second and third steps is, when challenged, do you speak your mind or forever hold your peace?

Zen discipline contributes to professionalism in balancing the use of speech and silence. The Unmoving Mind adjusts the use of words and of no-words to fit a specific situation and rearrange or escape altogether from a framework that becomes constraining and a source of oppression. Whether you are being expressive or reticent at any particular time should not be determined by pressures from outside forces but by self-control in selecting forms of expression conducive to positive change. It is your choice.

When both words and no-words fail, a more inventive form of White Collar Zen is required, which is found in the fourth step, the path of anti-structure. Awakening the Unmoving Mind empowers you to cross over invisible lines of hierarchy and division. One knows when to—and when not to—go beyond rules of protocol and procedure through unconventional actions.

Structure creates a standard framework that instructs people how to behave in a way that leads to cooperation and harmony.

This can be motivating and liberating, as in the strict discipline of the Zen monastic lifestyle, yet it also has the potential to be constraining and lead to regimentation and rigidity.

True power is based on the authority of ideas and ideals. You are enabled, with sufficient preparation, to leap out of the cookie-cutter mold. Zen masters are known in traditional accounts for tossing or kicking away important symbols, as well as scolding and slapping their rivals and students. They are even seen committing or instructing followers to commit destructive acts, like cutting off people's limbs or slicing cats in half, to make a point about questioning authority that is imposed arbitrarily or without genuine accord among all parties.

Cutting through structure involves taking risks but can be appropriate and conducive to progressive interaction and growth. This is true so long as you are not taking advantage or revealing contempt, but displaying genuine humility and willingness to undergo self-scrutiny and self-criticism. Since the anti-structural approach is unpredictable and has an edge of defiance, it may result in excesses and abuse or be perceived as anarchic or arbitrary. White Collar Zen, in bringing the Unmoving Mind into the new frontier of the contemporary workplace, strives for a balanced attitude that strengthens rather than defeats structure based on discipline that inspires creativity.

Entrance Through Two Gates

The delicate balance between structure and anti-structure is expressed in classical as well as modern teachings. In sixth-century China, the first patriarch of Zen, a monk named **Bodhidharma**, wrote that there are two gates for entering the Dharma (Buddhist truth of enlightenment). One gate is the patient use of reason and the study of scriptures in a formal monastic setting. The other gate is the practice of individual meditation, often in solitude or retreat, to trigger a sudden awakening. Eventually, the act of meditation came to be associated with the study of koans. Enigmatic, thought-provoking koans epitomize the ingenuity of classical Zen Buddhism in sharpening the Mind and bringing out its maximum utility.

At a high point in the appropriation of Zen in America in the 1950s, Alan Watts in the essay, "Beat Zen, Square Zen, and Zen" described two new, contemporary approaches that echoed this distinction between gradual and sudden enlightenment. First, **Beat Zen** is associated with a spontaneous spiritual awakening as evidenced in the creativity of poets, musicians, and performers. Beat writers like Jack Kerouac and Gary Snyder spent their summers as fire lookouts on lonely, lost peaks of the great Northwest, replicating the solitude of mountain pilgrims in traditional China and Japan.

The Beat approach integrates a Zen consciousness featuring irreverent, anti-authoritarian attitudes and lifestyle with deliberately enigmatic expressions of an experience of awakening. According to Allen Ginsberg's seminal prose-poem (or "proem"), *Howl*:

- *I saw the best minds of my generation destroyed by*
   madness, starving hysterical naked...
   angelheaded hipsters burning for the ancient heavenly
   connection to the starry dynamo in the machinery of
   night...

While admiring the way Beat Zen captures the defiance of structure, Watts finds this approach is a shade too self-conscious, subjective and strident to have the flavor of real Zen. According to Watts,

- *If you wish to spend some time hopping freight cars and digging Charlie Parker music, it is after all a free country.*

But he recommends that you can learn more about the classical teaching of Zen by training in an authentic Japanese monastery.

The second category is **Square Zen**, which does its best to emulate traditional rituals, given modern changes in gender roles and social values. Square Zen is practiced both by the immigrant, Japanese ethnic community and by non-Asians exploring varieties of mysticism. However, in striving for intellectual authenticity and authority, Square Zen, according to Watts, often misses the creative inspiration and insight of the Unmoving Mind. The "how" or style of doing things is just as important as the "what" or substance of activity. In Kabbala, the Jewish mystical tradition, there is a saying that a disciple can learn more from watching a teacher tie his shoes than reading all the scriptures and commentaries in the Talmud.

Knowing that both the Beat or anti-structural and the Square or structural approaches are capable of creating freedom or bondage, White Collar Zen tries to avoid extremes by demonstrating agility in choosing whether to function within structure or outside it. It maneuvers flexibly between the most compelling aspects of the complementary paths, working within the rules yet also bending but not flouting or violating them.

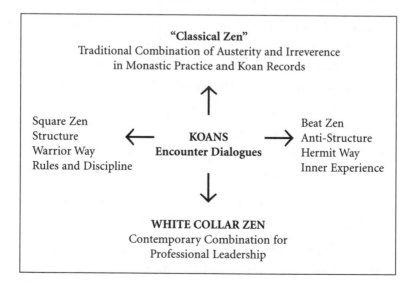

The key to understanding the calm composure coupled with spontaneous flexibility of the Unmoving Mind is the koan. Koans, or records of "Encounter dialogues," were first preserved in China and Japan in dozens of collections created from the eleventh through the fourteenth centuries. At that time, many brilliant though eccentric and unpredictable Zen masters emerged alongside widespread belief in the power of supernatural entities, like magical animals and ghosts, to control sacred domains. This period also saw the proliferation of Art of War strategies for warriors based on the virtues of attentiveness derived from heightened spiritual awareness.

Zen masters used the folklore and military imagery embedded in Chinese culture to make a point about the struggle to prove their spiritual ability through competitions or "Dharma combats." These are a special form of dialogue, based on the Encounter model, which takes place between teachers and disciples as well as other kinds of rivals and trainees. The aim of the Encounter dialogue is to pit Mind against Mind, with no holds barred and may the best person win! The main examples were often composed to resemble ritual contests between shamans or wizards and gods and demons. They also often create an atmosphere of military intrigue, as Zen masters were compared to generals mapping their plans of battle.

Koan records capture conversations and nonverbal exchanges that show how masters sought to break through barriers of language and hierarchy imposed by social and religious structures. The Encounter dialogue evokes what Zen calls,

- *Strange deeds and extraordinary words.*

Genuine creativity that derives from intuitive awareness beyond logic cannot be contained within the regulated use of words that reflects mainstream organizational structures. Originality explodes in ways that transgress and disrupt the conventional and ordinary.

In a fascinating example, master **Pai-chang** requires his two leading followers, the head monk and an upstart named **Kuei-shan**, to
compete. The winner of the contest will be awarded the prize of
the abbacy of his own mountain temple. Master Pai-chang puts his
disciples in a double bind by asking them to describe an object,

• *Without calling it a pitcher and without not calling it a pitcher.*

This type of absurd command compels those challenged to go
beyond ordinary words and yet communicate in a spontaneous
and convincing fashion. One must react immediately and without hesitation, letting nothing interfere with an instinctive response. Generally, no one beats the master, yet he is the first to
admit defeat if and when bested.

The head monk's answer to the question about the pitcher is,
"It can't be called a wooden clog." He attempts to fight fire with
fire by giving a response that is just as absurd as the query, yet his
reliance on language misses the mark. The upstart Kuei-shan's
response is to kick over the pitcher and simply walk away from
the scene. His demonstrative gesture prevails and he goes on to
lead the new monastery.

Kuei-shan kicking over the water pitcher.

Kuei-shan's gesture is one of the most renowned cases of an anti-structural expression in Zen annals. It shows a willingness to break away from conventional hierarchy and patterns of discourse. If you want to stand out you cannot do the same as everyone else. You need to have the courage to try new approaches that might be perceived as offbeat or "crazy." This is the risk taken to be innovative. Failure to seize the opportunity to be uniquely inventive will in the end stymie communal achievements. Taking the risk is not an end in itself and is effective only as long as it integrates individuality and eccentricity with a commitment to teamwork and the completion of group goals.

The koan narrative shows the point of the fourth step of an Encounter. When both words and no-words fall short of communicating, a genuine sense of self-confidence and creativity beyond speaking and silence, based on integrity and inner discipline, allows for deftness and innovation in breaking the mold of hierarchical structure. Before doing things this way, it is necessary to have exhausted other avenues and to be certain about the merits and reasonableness of your approach. Kuei-shan's act of breaking down structures, which gains him a leadership role in the monastic system, works because it takes place at the appropriate time and context, without seeming arbitrary or renegade.

Dilemma and distress often arise from the immediate environment and structure that surround us. With everything on the line, one must be able to box his or her way out of a corner at any moment. Conventional hierarchical structure is shifted to put an emphasis on awareness rather than status. A line from the film, *Training Day*, describes how freewheeling self-confidence requires you to play a more complicated game that calls for a greater grasp of strategy,

- *This is chess. It ain't checkers.*

In responding to the challenge, it is important not to stay fixed on a particular style. Every situation is unique and demands a reaction suited to those circumstances. No one way of doing things is strictly incorrect or correct. Each approach must be evaluated in relative terms. Unconventionality functions in what Taoist philosopher Chuang Tzu calls the,

- *Hinge of the Way.*

In operating at this hinge, you can move back and forth at will in response to shifting tides. That is why Lin-chi refers to the overcoming of obstructions as becoming the,

- *True Person Without Rank.*

Therefore, Zen teachings yield several important lessons for developing management and motivational skills by showing how to:

1. Transform dysfunctional conflicts based on petty turf battles and ego-induced confrontations into **mutually beneficial negotiations** characterized by shared purposes and cooperation.
2. Develop an atmosphere that **promotes and sustains creativity and spontaneity** while also providing order and regularity as in the traditional Zen monastic system, which is one of the most highly structured settings in the world yet allows for or requires outrageous, irreverent, even blasphemous behavior as found among the creative geniuses of classical Zen masters.
3. Recognize when it is useful or necessary to break the rules, and demonstrate **distinctively innovative unconventional behavior** or anti-structure.
4. Create appropriate conditions so that followers are inspired to challenge and surpass their leaders, who do not just rest on their laurels as models of authority but are willing to **acknowledge the merit of disciples** who surpass them.

Yet, it may seem unrealistic or even silly to think of modeling your behavior in a contemporary professional context on the outrageous, seemingly disrespectful action of a medieval Zen master. Professionalism does not necessarily leave room for, and indeed generally disallows and disqualifies, the anti-structural dimension. How about the rebellious Marlon Brando's motorcycle-riding character in the film, *The Wild One*? When asked what he was rebelling against, Brando replied,

- *Whaddya got?*

Is that the attitude to emulate? You may think to yourself, let me try that and see how far I get. Maybe they would make you head of a new division (or monastery)! On the other hand, without making the effort to be innovative, how much would you be likely to achieve?

PART TWO

Mountains Are Not Mountains: Transforming Conflict into Opportunity

First there is a mountain,
Then there is no mountain,
Then there is...

> Donovan

CHAPTER THREE

Everybody Must Get Foxed

Promotion Commotion

A CCORDING TO THE TEACHINGS of classical Buddhism, life is characterized by suffering or a fundamental sense of dissatisfaction similar to the anxiety (or *Angst*) of modern psychology and philosophy. **Dukkha**, the term for suffering, literally means being out of joint or off balance as, for example, when a wheel is out of alignment and throws off the movement of the vehicle it carries. The Buddhist view is not pessimistic, but reflects a deep understanding of the ebb and flow of life. Running late, missing a deadline, or being held up by some delay—these mundane experiences are not only frustrating in themselves, but reveal the instability and fragility that underlie our ordinary existence and can be manifested at any time.

The root of anxiety is self-interest in the pejorative sense: attachment or grasping for what we cannot attain and pushing away that which we do not desire. Buddhism teaches that anxiety is generally experienced in one of two ways:

- As <u>Absence</u>—*something is not in the world that you feel should be there, or a person, position, or possession that you desire remains an elusive goal.*

45

- *As <u>Presence</u>—something is in the world that you feel should not be there, or you are faced with an unwanted item or obstacle that is difficult to eliminate.*

In the professional sphere, a prime example of anxiety based on absence occurs when an expected promotion is denied or delayed. An unwanted or burdensome assignment exemplifies anxiety created by presence. In the first case, you feel that something you deserve and have been anticipating or counting on has been taken away. In the second case, something undesirable or overwhelming has been foisted on you. Either your ship has not yet come in or you have missed the boat.

According to Buddhism, whether you receive something you do not want or are thwarted in claiming what you expect, you should resist the futility and despair of endless grasping. Recognizing that no matter how hard you try, the long arm of Yama, the lord of decay, decline, and death, can never be evaded. You can, however, alter your attitude toward the constant flux by applying Zen strategies of maintaining equilibrium and concentration while being active and assertive each spontaneous moment. Understanding the syndromes of absence and presence can help transform petty turf battles into opportunities for constructive negotiation. Getting past denial and accepting the reality of presence or of absence is the necessary first step for gaining control of your state of mind.

Consider the problem of suffering through absence. Suppose you are being actively considered for a promotion to the position of director of a dynamic, expanding division, an outstanding job that could also be a steppingstone for future advancement. Your main competitor is an admired colleague who is already a cut above you on the corporate ladder. It looks like a win-win situation. You have a recent track record of first-rate accomplishments and the apparent respect of the vice president and her board of advisors. If your colleague gets the job then you in all likelihood will be promoted into his present position. Either way, you feel you are destined and determined to move up.

The interviews for the position are finished. The time has come and nothing can stop the train pulling into the station, right? But then a postponement in the promotion process is announced. No one gets the nod. Everything is being reevaluated. Are you really surprised and shocked, or did you know all along to expect the unexpected, or not to expect anything at all? In the novel *Lost Horizon*, the hero's illusions go up in smoke when he suddenly realizes that he had been deceived into believing in a false utopia,

- *It came to him that a dream had dissolved, like all too lovely things, at the first touch of reality.*

Conditions leading to the announcement undoubtedly were developing over a long time. You failed to perceive this because the dominant factors had not yet coalesced. Awakenings are often rude. Perhaps you have been working on a project by planning, brainstorming, networking, and researching, all the while feeling a vague uneasiness or a faint awareness that something may be wrong, but without taking time to pinpoint the cause. Once the problem appears, oversights, discrepancies, and misguided efforts long neglected come to light with a vengeance.

But why has the boss acted this way? Has she lost confidence in you and your colleague, or is she trying to set up a different way to assess the candidates that may (or may not) work for (or against) your interests? Has some unsuspected deficiency in your credentials been discovered? Were you misled or betrayed by somebody who inflated your hopes or undercut your cause? Or has an attractive outside candidate suddenly emerged from the wings? You reflect on the First Law of Employment Dynamics: When you are the outsider there is an inside candidate who has the deal sewed up before you ever get the interview. But the opposite is also the case. When you are on the inside, there inevitably seems to be a highly qualified outsider who, people say, offers everything you can and possibly more.

The Second Law states that eagerly waiting the desired result is sure to kill the deal, but the moment your mind relinquishes the thought of what could be, then good news comes to you (at least some of the time). In Japan, this is known as relying on Other Power (a path of devotion)—recognizing that there are times when you let things happen of their own accord. This attitude complements the Zen approach of Self Power, according to which you and you alone are the force that is causing the change. Combining the two approaches, you know when to let go and when to push further, and do not get caught up in the trap of not knowing what you want or not wanting what you know. By examining all the possibilities of hope and disappointment to arrive at a balanced view of potential outcomes, you can avoid getting caught off guard by a surprise from either direction if you stay rooted firmly in perpetual planning that is flexible enough to take into account unforeseen setbacks.

When the news hits, however, the first thought is to go directly to the vice president as to inquire about the delay and request clarification of the status of the search. This approach is unlikely to yield useful information. A supervisor probably won't respond to a direct question unless there is a particular reason to keep candidates informed. In appearing interested solely in the promotion for yourself, you fail to demonstrate the professionalism that merits the upgrade or the "right stuff"—a focus on quality of work completed, with indifference toward personal outcome. The paradox is:

- *The more you claim the goal the less likely you are to impress. The less you assert your right the better your chances.*

You might also react by going over the supervisor's head, notifying the president of a grievance about procedures if you discover that the search was handled in a way that may not have followed company guidelines or precedents. While this might succeed in gaining attention, by not going through channels you fail to give the top brass the chance either to declare their intentions or remedy any breach of protocol. You risk appearing petty, vindictive, jealous, or prone to making unproductive complaints that upset the organization at several levels. A forced meeting with the highest administrator may simply seal your fate.

The real issue is not irregularities in protocol but how the vice president evaluates performances. You cannot effectively address the matter of how and why the assessment was made by raising a question about process, unless this is firmly supported by objective, quantitative criteria. If you are selling your house, a prospective buyer may try to back out of the deal by finding loopholes in the contract. It is not very likely that you could successfully sue a reluctant buyer to force him to complete the sale. Similarly, it is not usually prudent to complain about a manager whom you would like to promote you some day. Although it is a good idea to speak up for yourself, doing it this way can jeopardize future support.

Another alternative is to remain silent and see how things unfold. The risk is that patience without the firmness and steadiness of a clear purpose and direction may end in passivity or paralysis. This allows the status quo to preserve itself and prevail over your initiative. Seeming overly philosophical and resigned rather than lofty and transcendent will prove counterproductive if you end up standing by idly.

Compare this scenario with one that is based not on the absence of what is desired but the presence of something unwanted. Your supervisor walks into your office, closes the door, sits down, and asks about your family. He then hands you an assignment portfolio for a new project that requires a shift in priorities and carries high expectations for deliverable results under a tight deadline despite limited resources. He has decided that he wants you to oversee a small unit that is in difficulty. The unit has some highly qualified players but has lacked leadership and direction. The mission is to refashion the troubled group under your receivership, which is expected to end the fractiousness and lead to improved productivity.

Even though you will continue to be evaluated primarily for the main tasks in your job description, you will now be required to stretch your own time and your staff's energies to solve a set of problems that you did not create. It will be up to you to ease their pain, and in attending to a situation that requires diligent effort with little chance for a big payoff you may have to neglect the projects and priorities that you care about. As in the case of the promotion, you have probably seen this assignment coming for some time. The unit's strife was apparent, and it was likely that the organization would turn to you. Now that premonition has become reality and the sense of anxiety is palpable, you must be able to show some reaction on the spot without a chance to deliberate. If you request time to think things over, this will be considered a part of your response. The clock started ticking and the assessment of your performance got underway the moment the supervisor stepped into the room.

The thoughts running through your mind veer and swerve. Is the supervisor helping or hurting you? You hope this assignment is a vote of confidence and a grand opportunity to expand your base of power, and speculate that it may be a test to see if you are ready for bigger and better things. Yet you also wonder whether it represents some kind of punishment or a greasing of the skids. A sense of optimism can seem naïve and can easily turn to pessimism when hopes are dashed. Typically, you want increased support while supervisors want to see you making do with fewer resources.

When institutional structure imposes its weight, the message seems loud and clear: do not speak up or upset the applecart. But this may become an excuse to remain speechless, not due to thoughtful reflection, but simply because you feel no one is listening. At such a critical moment, the ups and downs of ordinary life give way to a more profound awareness of suffering. In this case anxiety is caused by the presence of something unwanted, but as with the promotion example the alternative responses seem rooted either in passivity or aggressive action.

One possibility is a nod of acceptance to demonstrate an ability to take things in stride and make the best of any circumstance,

- *Sure, I'll do it; or, Great, I'll see what I can do with this.*

But, if this affirmation reflects intimidation and trepidation rather than choice and self-determination, the show of cooperation may prove hollow. A friend once told the story that, put in a similar situation and asked, "Can you handle this?"

- *The words "Of course, sir," were out of my mouth before I had even a moment's reflection.*

Another aspect of the affirmative approach is to respond quickly and aggressively, asking just how you will be expected to undertake the assignment successfully and still be able to complete your other projects. Yet this response may appear to show resistance to the workload. If it has a trace of insincerity or is worded wrongly, you betray a lack of confidence that produces friction or conflict. If you project that you are not capable of doing the work, the supervisor may begin to scrutinize your regular job performance more skeptically.

Or, you can try not to commit yourself right off, in order to buy time to think over the full significance of the assignment after the heat of the moment passes. Then you will be able to craft a detailed response that expresses questions and concerns or articulates a plan of action reflecting your own interests while satisfying the demands of your supervisor and his superiors. However, by delaying, you may end up stuck with some condition or contingency that is unacceptable yet irrevocable. By the time you raise an objection, the supervisor's reply may be,

• *Too late now. Why didn't you bring that up before?*

Senpai had a friend who was called to interview for an entry-level position he desperately wanted. The employer's explanation of the schedule seemed overly casual and somewhat confusing. The friend tried to lighten the atmosphere and get things back on track with a quip, "Could you possibly be a little vaguer than that?" This was an inappropriate and ineffective use of anti-structure because he had not yet entered the gate of structure. Needless to say, he didn't get the job and the gateway remained closed.

The alternative responses to the assignment example have potential strengths; one asserts a degree of independence and spontaneity, while the other buys time for reflection and shows flexibility. They also have the drawback of either failing to make changes or antagonizing the boss, respectively. Both reveal an inability to seize the challenge as an opportunity rather than an obstacle or problem. If you treat the offer of the assignment as a routine matter without paying sufficient attention or exaggerate its difficulty, you find yourself trapped in a no-win situation. By failing to understand the reasons why you lack leverage in this situation, you are unable to gain authority through constructive dialogue and negotiation.

Think about the interplay of these responses. One reaction seems quick and forceful, while the other seems slower and more passive. In one case, you may complain too much, and in the other you do not appear to express yourself at all. But in both instances there is an instant of hesitation and a lack of resiliency. In that single moment of time in which you weigh and evaluate all of the implications of your attitudes toward the assignment, pro and con, a subtle but wide-as-a-highway gap has opened up between the action taken toward you and your inability to respond immediately, which imperils the chance to influence what happens next.

Mulling things over and thinking carefully before acting is not necessarily detrimental. You naturally want to be consulted and have the time and freedom to discuss matters with colleagues and staff. But if you do not have a knack for the ability to react with spontaneity that encompasses a careful assessment minus delays, you can say "sayonara" to chances for an effective response. How do you stop forfeiting opportunities and instead activate them here and now? The goal of Zen is to develop a preemptive approach, in which the ability to act first becomes second nature.

Rainy-Day Reflections

Faced with disappointment, it is all too easy to fall into a pattern of negativity. The day after receiving troubling news about a promotion, you may walk into a planning session and realize that your voice is not being heard, your ideas are not given credence, and your state of awareness is dimmed. You are preoccupied with the question, What went wrong? Look around you. It is written all over their faces, isn't it?

Maybe not. Maybe you are just imagining this, retreating into a shell of paranoia. If you think people react solely on the basis of your most recent successes or failures, this will feed anxiety, creating a vicious cycle of inner turmoil and outward misunderstanding. How did you end up so out of tune with yourself and unaligned with your community of peers who help determine your reputation and the recognition you receive?

Why does it seem that the more you try to achieve a goal through direct means, the more elusive and evasive it becomes? In the words of a Paul Simon song,

- *You know the nearer your destination, the more you're slip, slidin' away.*

You seek to understand why such a gap has opened up between what you expect and what occurs. Were you trying to attain too much or underselling yourself and striving for far less than you could achieve? You might look for the source of the problem in a particular person or group. Amid the constraints and concerns of interpersonal relations, you may feel that you are being deceived or betrayed by forces on a higher or a lower level of the organizational chart.

There are people who, Buddha-like, help because they believe in your cause and others who become allies only because they feel they have something to gain. Furthermore, there may be those who appear to work against you, with only their own interest at heart. An apparent supporter may turn out to take advantage and wound your sense of dignity. Or a supervisor, who seems extremely positive so long as you are producing results from which he can benefit, suddenly turns cold. Sometimes the very people you have the most faith in, or who appear unquestionably trustworthy, may suddenly seem culpable or responsible for your decline. When their behavior is examined, however, it often becomes clear that they are well meaning yet simply have a different agenda or sense of timing. Detractors may also be revealed as hidden Buddhas who only seem standoffish because they are committed to recognizing and rewarding merit without regard for personal interest.

Senpai had an associate who appeared bright, cheerful, and cooperative just up to the point where they achieved what they wanted. Then they, or the elusive, intangible sense of resolve and commitment to a project they represented, vanished into thin air, never to be seen or heard from again. The faucet was turned off and nothing flowed from it. This failure spoke poorly of Senpai, who would find himself in a double bind of being left in the lurch with responsibility for making up the associate's workload while also covering for their lack of follow-through.

Visualize a small box sitting on your desk. If you look down, you can see the top clearly. You also see at least a significant part of three of the box's sides. The fourth side can be seen if you rotate the box or if you get up and walk around to view the other side. It is accessible but only if either your or its position is changed. What you cannot see at all is the bottom of the box, where the sun never shines, whose hiddenness may give it a mysterious allure. When you finally are able to turn the box over and see the underside for what it is, you may be aghast to discover that it is dark and corroded. It is as if you suddenly realize that termites are devouring the foundation of your home. By reconciling to this discovery, you can begin to exterminate the scourge.

In Zen folklore, spirit possession or the invasion of your psychic space by a magical, shape-shifting Fox that passes itself off as human is an infallible sign of delusion. This usually afflicts someone who has a tendency to stray from the straight-and-narrow path. The Fox is great at pretending to be real. Although there are bound to be telltale signals of its true nature, as the ensnarement unfolds the victim rejects warning signals, including those offered by a neutral outsider. Like the chorus in a Greek tragedy, there is usually an observer present, who is unaffected by the Fox's guile and guises and offers a word of caution that goes unheeded. Observers may be supportive although their power to bring about change is much more limited than that of a Buddha. Yet, the victim usually imagines that the observer is merely jealous, and ignores the signs of illusion and deception swirling about. In traditional folklore, a warning to beware is the very last thing the entranced person wants to hear while in the thrall of illusion. Nevertheless, the observer's clarity and insight based on the ability to see all sides evenhandedly offers a crucial lesson in spiritual awareness.

Eventually, the person undergoing an infatuation or bewitchment comes to a moment of discovery. When an all-too-obvious betrayal becomes impossible to ignore, this unwelcome insight liberates the mind from the hold of ignorance and attachment. In folklore, this happens when the fox's tail lying just beneath the kimono or robe is exposed and the shape-shifter reverts to its original vulpine or nonhuman status. The revelatory moment leaves the victim to struggle with the realization that they have been hampered by so much deception.

Fox shrine at Toyokawa Inari temple in Tokyo.

In the case of the delayed promotion or the unwanted assignment, is there a Fox behind the disturbance? Why did the supervisor change her mind? Perhaps an anonymous colleague spoke
against you to the committee while pushing his or her own agenda?
Will you ever learn the identity of a colleague who has a knack
for seizing on the vulnerability and weakness of others?

Sensing a Fox, however, is actually a sign that you have fallen
into a state of disappointment, discouragement, and disillusion.
A friend of Senpai was devastated when a colleague with whom
she had been closely associated seemed to undercut her. The two
of them were preparing for a breakthrough project. She had the
expertise and would do the lion's share of the research, whereas
he had the influence and did the networking, especially in pre-
senting their file to the appropriate supervisor.

The day came when their project was to get the hearing they
had been hoping for. She waited for him to return from the meeting to call her at 4:00 PM with the results. The phone rang at

exactly 4:00 but it turned out to be someone else. This seemed like an odd coincidence. By 5:30 there was still no call from the colleague. Senpai's friend suspected her colleague had claimed all the credit. To paraphrase Dylan,

- *They'll fox you, and then they'll say "good luck,"*
  They'll fox you, when you get hit by a truck.

The Fox's casual indifference to your plight resembles, but is fundamentally different from, that of a lofty Hermit who is beyond the cares of the world. But it turned out the colleague had learned of a new level of complexity in planning and was busy consulting with other parties before he did eventually get back to Senpai's friend.

In *Casablanca*, lead character Rick played by Humphrey Bogart is devastated when by surprise he sees his former lover (Ingrid Bergman), who had jilted him in Paris. Reminiscing, while their favorite song is being played on the piano, he utters the words of the single most famous scene in the history of film,

- *Play it, Sam. Play it again.*

As the plot thickens, Rick learns that Bergman's character had deserted him out of loyalty to her husband, a leader of the Nazi resistance movement, who was freed from prison. By the end of the story, however, neither Rick nor the viewer is completely clear about her intentions or whether she has been manipulating his feelings for ulterior motives, whether noble or not. Was she Fox or Buddha?

To use a simple metaphor, perhaps you have reached for a chocolate chip cookie without really paying attention and picked up a raisin cookie by mistake. So long as the cookie is just sitting there its real quality is unknown. You cannot tell what a cookie tastes like from touching, looking at, or even smelling it. Whether it is appealing or repellent cannot be determined until the moment you bite into it. Once you take a bite it is too late to avoid an unpleasant taste. In the immortal words of Forest Gump,

- *Life is like a box of chocolates; you never know what you're going to get.*

The inseparability of Fox and Buddha is highlighted in Zen tales, which show that the Fox and the Buddha often manifest in similar guises and dis-guises. For strategic purposes, they conceal their motives and appear as something they are not. The real intention of allies and adversaries alike lies beneath the surface.

The Fox poses as a supporter to get what she wants. The greater the Fox's ambition, the more she tries to appear like a helpful Buddha. Fooling you is what being a Fox, who does not want its mischief told or its methods divulged, is all about. However, an observer with nothing to lose can look at the situation objectively and may have been aware of the Fox all along. Borrowing from the Fox's repertoire of duplicitous techniques, the Buddha poses as neutral or impartial so as not to appear to play favorites. The Buddha depends on parables and allegories, but cannot always ensure the transmitting of his message is done properly or to the desired effect.

Self as Frenemy

In the typical possession story, when the Fox is discovered a priest or shaman is called upon to banish the demonic spirit by chanting a mantra or copying a passage from a scripture. Following the exorcism, a fox corpse is found in the basement of the house, or a pack of foxes can be seen scurrying behind the temple or to the side of the battlefield. This serves as tangible evidence in the realm of physical reality of the elimination of the mischievous spirit in the invisible realm.

Fox folklore gives Zen Buddhist literature and ritual a mythological dimension. Shifts and changes in human affairs are explained by the actions of supernatural beings: ghosts and goblins, spirits and sprites, divinities and demons. If accepted at face value, this plays into the human tendency to look outside for the cause of suffering rather than scrutinizing your own actions.

However, the desire to blame external factors for one's woes is the sign of a weak spirit and an obstacle to progress. In the face of difficulties, delays, and defeats, it is crucial not to become stubborn and inflexible, fixated on the impossibility of success or on revenge for apparent wrongs.

It takes skill to be able to tell apart the possibilities, to expose the Fox while uncovering the Buddha. On the one hand, knowing who is and who is not a Fox requires the ability that only a Fox can have, as in the Zen saying,

- *It takes a Fox to know a Fox.*

But, the aim of Zen is not to leave things standing in the midst of deception. Zen recognizes that the appearance of the Fox symbolizes giving in to temptation, which is due to a lack of self-control. The overcoming of temptation is also due to the self, which has the ability to regain control. Seeing the Fox for what it really is requires the wisdom of a Buddha. Therefore, it must also be the case that,

- *It takes a Buddha to know a Buddha.*

This is something only you can do for yourself.

According to a saying from the Hindu scripture, the *Bhagavad Gita*, about the role of "frenemy,"

- *Self is the friend of self, and self is the enemy of self.*

You cannot control or predict how others will act or react. But, whether your response is swift and decisive or slow and observant, you have the ability to master your own actions and reactions. Your attitudes and deeds will earn a reputation either for impeccability that wins advancement and acclaim or for incapacity leading to stagnation and frustration. You are your own

best friend when you cultivate and perfect your strengths to continually surpass expectations. As the Buddha instructed his disciples near the time of his death,

- *Be lamps unto yourselves.*

The freedom of the Unmoving Mind is a dormant potential that is
activated through your own efforts and no one else's. In a Zen verse,

- *There is nothing lacking in you,*
  You are no different from the Buddha.

In the nineteenth century, Walt Whitman was aware of early
English translations of Asian mystical writings when he wrote
the following:

- *Stop this day and night with me and you shall possess the*
  origin of all poems,
  You shall possess the good of the earth and sun...there are
  millions of suns left,
  You shall no longer take things at second or third
  hand....nor look through the eyes of the dead, nor feed
  on the spectres in books,
  You shall not look through my eyes either, nor take things
  from me,
  You shall listen to all sides and filter them from yourself.

Developing the ability to serve as a "filter," the self takes in all
sides and rapidly evaluates pros and cons in a fair and reasonable
way. This gives you the equilibrium and fortitude to control reactions to the vicissitudes of life. Self as filter reacts to unpredictable and unstable circumstances with swift and effective
judgments or decisions.

    You and you alone can choose whether to give in to despon-
dency and overreliance on others or to develop flexibility, nimbleness, and perspicacity. Do not take anyone else's word. According
to a Zen saying,

- *Awakening to the true Self is self-awakening, not awakening caused by something outside the self.*

The Fox folklore of Zen should not be taken to mean that the world of external forces is an entirely separate, autonomous realm with which we interact. Rather, it serves as a metaphor for an inner state of mind. As modern Western thinkers and writers from Carl Jung to James Joyce, Franz Kafka, and Eugene O'Neill recognize, how things appear on the outside cannot be separated from our inner thoughts and fears. We project our state of mind onto external reality. The Fox is a very powerful figment of the imagination that arises on the borderline between perception and fantasy— in a realm we call the Twilight Zone. Our task on both external and internal planes is to overcome deception and falsehood by realizing clarity and truth.

Alfred Hitchcock's film *Vertigo*, a haunting masterpiece of intrigue and obsession, depicts the intertwining planes of reality. The tragic antihero, Scottie, played by Jimmy Stewart, must face his fear of heights over and over again in the most agonizing ways. In the climactic scene, he looks down from the church tower, not knowing whether he is being saved or betrayed by one of two maddeningly attractive women, both played by Kim Novak. The camera shows a spiral staircase extending ever downward as Scottie's anxiety mounts. The poster for the film depicts Scottie caught in a labyrinthine spiral that evokes the image of an eye. The eye symbolizes the way others are judging Scottie's psychological descent. For the filmgoer, who is as perplexed as Scottie by the mysterious unfolding of events and characters, this image symbolizes his or her own mind's eye following and recoiling from what is happening to the antihero. The spiral image seen in the staircase is not the depiction of an external object but the illumination of the state of mind of Scottie's inner turmoil.

In the Japanese film *Ugetsu*, another eminent movie from the 1950s, exorcism as an external ritual symbolizes repentance as

internal self-reflection. During wartime, Genjuro, a humble crafts-
man, abandons his wife and takes up residence with a beautiful,
seductive Fox in a huge mansion on the outskirts of town after
she buys some of his pottery. A priest spots him walking downtown while he is shopping for a gift and, sensing that something
is wrong, offers to provide him with spiritual protection by painting sacred letters on his body. After retuning to the house to confront the ghost and accidentally setting it ablaze, the husband
stumbles outside and is horrified to see that the mansion where
he thinks he has been dwelling is in reality a burnt-out hovel, while
the sheriff is ready to arrest him for vagrancy. Repentant, he re-
solves to return to his real home and make amends with his wife,
whom he finds waiting there to receive him. But it is only another
ghost. She has died in the interim. Following this double dose of
disillusionment, in the end Genjuro finds an awakening and
achieves peace of mind by communicating with the spirit of his
lost wife as he goes about raising their son.

My respected senior colleague, Senpai, once managed one of
the main units that was preparing for a major external audit. Most
employees were too low on the totem pole to be much involved
in this process, but were aware that intense pressure was building
for several weeks leading up to the day of the evaluation. Senpai
saw that the chief of one of the other units looked to the occasion
as a grand opportunity for his own personal advancement. This
unit leader was playing an important role in preparations and
planning, and saw himself competing with Senpai for the attention and kudos of their supervisor.

Senpai knew what was coming a mile away. The rival associate
was focusing solely on the efforts of his own unit and disregard-
ing avenues for teamwork and consensus building with the other
leaders. Senpai, on the other hand, was constructing bridges and
alliances. The supervisor and his aides sensed the associate's self-
indulgence and began to let him drift away, leaving him out of

important meetings and, worse, repressing off-the-cuff insider remarks when he was around. Therefore, he was not aware of some last-minute maneuverings that would be critical during the most heated moments when the evaluators were present. Others who were watching closely could feel that something was about to go wrong but had no way of anticipating what it would be and little recourse or leverage to speak up with a warning.

D-Day arrived. The ten leaders in the group lined up their files, but there was also an "eleventh file." The supervisor's idea was that this special file would be there, ready and waiting, but was not to be cited unless a certain kind of questioning came up, that is, until the proper signal was given. Refraining from going to this file at almost any cost was one of the little messages that Senpai's rival associate had not received, and he went ahead and opened up that file at an inopportune moment. For months afterwards he was reeling, swearing that he'd been framed. He suspected that other leaders benefited from his blunder, and was wary of the supervisor who had left him out of the loop as well as underlings who might have given him some warning. But Senpai felt he should have taken his cue from the Jimmy Buffet lyric (paraphrased):

- *Some people say there's another to blame,*
  But I know, it's my own damn fault.

Zen suggests that you are your own worst enemy when you fail to exhibit your strengths for reasons of convenience, ignorance, fatigue, or desperation. This state is referred to in koan commentaries as,

- *Pulling the bow after the thief has fled.*

This refers to an unproductive and delayed reaction through which opportunities are lost or squandered. Yet Senpai assured his team that the associate's work was as creative and innovative as anyone's and some day this would shine through. To develop confidence,

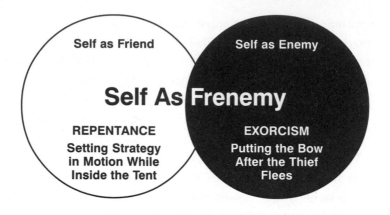

it is necessary to rise above personal concerns and prevent them from causing you to become petty or vindictive. In Zen the knack for making things happen effortlessly is known as,

- *Setting strategy in motion while remaining in the tent.*

The contrast is often sharply drawn. It is not the case, however, that each of us follows only one of these paths consistently and misses the other one entirely. Rather, each of us as a total Self struggles to navigate and negotiate between the two conditions and can emerge as a winner or loser depending on the circumstances. There are many thieves representing our deficiencies that continue to get away, but there are also priceless gems symbolizing great possibilities waiting to be discovered. You cause your own suffering and are responsible for liberating yourself.

The Titanic Sails at Dawn

Somehow, Senpai missed seeing *Titanic* in the theater. When it arrived on cable, every time he turned on the TV, there was the same scene of Leonardo DiCaprio extending his arm to pull back Kate Winslet, who had started to throw herself over the bow of the ship. Senpai was working very late one night and about to send an e-mail message that he knew he would regret in retrospect. Turning on the TV, he encountered the scene once again and realized it was a perfect representation of the self helping the self while on the edge of harming the self, or going from pulling the bow too late to setting strategy in motion.

In the mythical worldview, an exorcism is necessary to unmask the Fox, but metaphorically, it represents a process by which a new level of self-awareness is attained. There is no need for an intermediary to take the role of exorcist, because the Self bears full responsibility for undertaking introspection and repentance. Rather than feeling blindsided and focusing on the actions of others, investigate the hidden causes of your own behavior. Scottish poet Robert Burns wrote that we need to "see ourselves as others see us":

- *O wad some Power the giftie gie us*
  To see oursels as ithers see us!
  It wad frae mony a blunder free us,
  An' foolish notion...

Seeing yourself objectively enables a profound sense of self-criticism that will prevent you from making the same mistakes over and over again.

To change bad habits or faulty patterns of behavior, Zen advises that repentance uplifts and elevates by examining the depths of the problem from a lofty, transcendental view. Through repentance, intentions are purified and relationships become free of misunderstandings based on self-centered motives. Many people who have narrowly escaped death report experiencing a crucial turning point in which their whole life flashes before them. In a single instant of repentance, they recall episodes and conversations that would otherwise remain lost forever. This is a bit like cleaning out your old car in preparation to trade it in for a new one. You start finding all kinds of coins, papers, and other odd objects in every nook and cranny where they had lain forgotten.

The *Tibetan Book of the Dead* describes in extremely graphic and gruesome imagery the process of repentance during purgatory:

- *At this time you will be very frightened and terrified, and you will tremble and lie, saying, "I have not sinned." Then the Lord of Death will say, "I will look in the mirror of karma," and when he looks in the mirror all your sins and virtues will suddenly appear in it clearly and distinctly, so although you have lied it is of no use. Then the Lord of Death will drag you by a rope tied round your neck, and cut off your head, tear out your heart, pull out your entrails, lick your brains, drink your blood, eat your flesh and gnaw your bones.*

Similarly, in Charles Dickens' *A Christmas Carol*, Scrooge is forced to face in a momentary flash a comprehensive overview of his whole life in its past, present, and future manifestations, and to realize how he could have avoided and corrected the errors of his ways all along.

Are you able to tell a Buddha from a Fox? Yes, according to Zen, through the power of self-reflection. You seize the opportunity to stand outside of yourself and see all the various flaws and foibles in their multiple manifestations and implications:

- *The endeavor to awaken to self without awakening others is selfish, whereas the attempt to awaken others without awakening to self is powerless.*

According to a Zen saying, "The sword that gives life is the sword that kills," and the opposite is also true. In that vein, there are folk tales about Buddhas who take the form of foxes in order to teach a moral lesson. For example, a Buddha-cum-Fox saves a prince from falling in a ditch. The royal personage then thinks to himself,

- *If even a fox behaved with such compassion, I must do the same in the treatment of my subjects.*

It is said that the Buddha attained enlightenment while sitting under a tree, in a deep meditative trance. He stayed in this state for a number of weeks and did not move. A Naga (serpent or dragonlike entity with magical, shape-shifting powers like those of the Fox) came and held its head over the Buddha like an umbrella, to shelter him from the rain. Various creatures helped nourish the Buddha so that he was able to withstand the taunts of Mara, the Demon. He was offered several temptations, but remained steady. The actions of the Naga show that chaotic energy and rogue elements can be elevated and purified into a force that is then activated as an agency of protection.

Zen literature uses the epithet "Wild Fox Spirit!" to criticize inauthentic monks who ostensibly sought a state of egolessness but demonstrated arrogance and conceit. At the same time, Zen temples often contain icons of foxes that serve as fertility symbols. In many folk tales, the Fox is transformed by a priest into an ally and protector of the spirit of the Buddha; the Fox is no longer Fox but a form of Buddha. A Fox appearing in a Zen temple signifies that the devious tendencies are tame and now resonate with the forces of wisdom. Therefore, referring to a monk as a "wild fox spirit" can be a foxy, tongue-in-cheek way of calling him a Buddha.

Now get back to work, you Wild Fox!

CHAPTER FOUR

The Greater the Doubt,
the Greater the Enlightenment

What Comes Down Must Go Up

SENPAI TOLD A STORY about his own experience on the path to enlightenment. As a young researcher, he was looked on as one of the best in his field and a leading candidate for an annual prize, with just one primary competitor. Or so he thought. Although he was considered the insider who had the backing of the judges and he believed himself to be the frontrunner, the result was a crushing defeat. It turned out that Senpai was not even a finalist; another candidate he thought of as a dark horse captured the award.

In defeat he was left only with suspicion, speculation, and lingering self-doubt. Senpai never learned what had taken place behind the scenes. He tried to be clear in his own mind about the borderline between what he knew for sure and what he could only guess at, while realizing that soon enough he would be facing some of the same rivals in other competitions.

As luck would have it, Senpai was called on to serve as an external evaluator of a project led by the recipient of the award. He examined the case carefully and objectively, and after extensive deliberation handed in a positive though constructively critical analysis. Readers of this evaluation who were aware of the rivalry were impressed by Senpai's handling of the assessment process, which focused on the merits of the project and did not reveal any sense of spite. Even the erstwhile rival acknowledged his indebtedness for Senpai's recommendations.

Some time later, Senpai got to know the person who won the competition. Looking back, he realized that the evaluation had been a defining moment on his own career path. It was a challenge that enabled him to prove his value. He had climbed out of the cave of dejection and into the fresh alpine air of professional dignity by realizing that positive deeds with long-range benefits would amply compensate for the defeat he had suffered.

Senpai's inner odyssey exemplifies the three stages of Elevation, Purification, and Activation (EPA):

(a) **Elevate feelings**—rise above conflict and confrontation through experiencing the Great Doubt.

(b) **Purify intentions**—free yourself from personal agendas by adopting the Hermit's way of transcendence to be clear, objective, and impartial.

(c) **Activate the Mind**—emerge from the quiet and solitude of contemplation and embrace the Warrior's way of incisive action.

He realized that an experience of doubt could call into question and release you from the stranglehold of assumptions and expectations. However, there is one kind of doubt that feeds hopelessness and a more profound kind that uplifts and transforms. It is crucial to distinguish one kind from the other, to activate the latter category while dissipating the effects of the deficient kind of doubt.

Senpai admitted that when news of the award first broke he felt in his gut an all-consuming anxiety and lack of confidence in his abilities and relations with colleagues. He recalled that as a boy, his older brother and friends went to a horror movie called *Them*, in which giant ants created by nuclear fallout were devouring people, and the kids all came home feverish with terror. Because his mom considered him too young to see the flick, he had stayed home where he watched a TV show in which an adventurer in some far-off land got stuck in quicksand. This gave him nightmares for weeks. The 1950s black-and-white special effects used for both the monsters and the exotic landscape were primitive. But nothing was scarier than the idea of being slowly but surely sucked down by quicksand, and the agonizing final moments as you see your end approaching and there is nothing you can do to stop it.

In Zen, the situation of being pulled ever downward by your emotions is known as ordinary doubt, which vacillates between shame-filled self-loathing and hostility. According to a koan commentary,

- *Letting it all go, or taking it all in? At first too high and then too low. When you realize the error of your ways, you should try to correct them. But how many people are capable of doing this?*

Ordinary doubt leads to a sense of despair. Throwing up your hands in disgust and disdain, you make no effort to investigate the source or extent of the problem. Without such a discovery, there can be no recovery.

If advancement is withheld, ordinary doubt leaves you feeling unsure whether you are capable of moving ahead or whether you are even able to assess your own qualifications. You are likely to swing in an unbalanced way between a stoic acceptance that rests on passive denial and the other extreme of a volatile, perhaps explosive and misdirected anger that leads to greater confusion. A subservient posture is ineffective because only a squeaky wheel gets oiled, and open complaint or an eruption of intense emotion can sometimes result in a short-term gain. Often you must speak up for yourself, but this can easily be perceived as self-aggrandizing if you give voice to personal agendas rather than promoting the values and interests of others. People may end up giving you what you want, in part to keep things under control. But showing a lack of patience and poise while breaking unwritten rules of hierarchical protocol is a misuse of anti-structure that betrays inner conflict and can trigger a Confrontation. Even if the case has merit, you squander chances for success by alienating colleagues who might have supported you. Instead, cultivate ways to call attention to your work without appearing defensive or hostile.

Unfulfilled goals or unwanted results create feelings of instability and inadequacy. The suspicion that your disappointment may have been caused by a Fox, whether in the form of a supervisor or a competitor, makes you hesitate and lose opportunities one by one. At first, you give others the benefit of the doubt. Then you turn in the other direction, but are troubled for distrusting them. You may even find that an observer, who has warned you to be cautious, is not altogether uninvolved and free of bias, so you become suspicious of his outlook as well. What do others have to gain from casting aspersion on you? Are they themselves immune from blame?

Once expectations have been dashed, you become prey to uncertainty as to whether you could really handle a promotion, yet you are also uncomfortable settling for your previous position. You continue to perform your job well, but this is mainly in the hope of landing another position, even if it means making a lateral move to salvage at least the illusion of upward mobility. If you are in sales, you want to avoid dealing with customers and move into management. A teacher wishes to escape the classroom to focus on research or administration, and a manager wants to move from an advisory to a policy-making role. If you finally do gain a new position, there is a fear that you may fall victim to the "Peter Principle" (according to which the reward for having perfected one set of skills is promotion to a different role for which you lack the experience or ability).

When Senpai wrote the evaluation of his rival's performance, he knew that just as he was examining another's credentials, the rival and his supporters were also scrutinizing him. There were also third-party observers sizing up the way Senpai assessed things. In this process, flaws are exposed if your evaluation reveals either too much emotion or puts a greater than necessary emphasis on abstraction and theory. The knowledge that you are being observed should not induce paralysis or panic, but rather should supply the motivation to enhance the clarity and lucidity of analysis.

A traditional folk song that evokes an endless series of external observers can also be used to describe an interior state of mind:

- *I wonder who's watchin' the one who's watchin' me?*
  And I wonder who's watchin' the one who's watchin' the one who's watchin' me,
  Who's watchin' the one who's watchin' the one who's watchin' the one who's watchin' the one who's watchin' the one who's watchin' me?

The situation of being caught in an infinite regress of doubting and questioning the basis of doubt is like the old Jackie Mason schtick. He used to be so uptight that when he sat in the stands at a football game and saw the players go into a huddle he assumed they were talking about him. But then he convinced himself that was a good thing.

At the time he was feeling the utmost frustration, Senpai came to the realization that he was behaving as a cocksure loner, certain that everyone must inevitably recognize his value. Part of his problem was an impulse toward complacency, which reflects a deep-rooted unwillingness to undertake fundamental change.

Overconfidence is actually a form of self-doubt, in which an arrogant attitude is a symptom of underlying anxiety. As Heraclitus wrote,

- *There is a greater need to extinguish arrogance than a blazing fire.*

Resting comfortably with the status quo and allowing things to stand pat, complacency prevails because it is the least amount of bother. William Osler, a leader in the early days of modern medicine and scientific experimentation, once said,

- *People do not make the effort to disprove what they suspect is wrong with the same vigor as when they try to prove what they hope is right.*

This is a tendency so typical of human nature that it infects Fox and Buddha alike. A koan commentary scoffs at a certain kind of monk whose arrogance leads to an utter lack of self-awareness,

- *He doesn't even know his shit stinks.*

When supervisors assign a low priority to an important project on which you have been laboring, seek out the reasons for this setback by means of self-criticism rather than appointing blame. Instead of denying what had already happened or refusing to accept what could not be helped, Senpai acknowledged the sense of being backed into a corner with no one and nowhere to turn. Devastated and disillusioned, he knew he was at an impasse with no way out and no means of stopping the world. A fire was burning and the alarm was blaring but the doors and windows were shut tight, the stairway was blocked, and the elevator broken.

This is the experience of the Great Doubt, which frees from entanglement and provides steadiness and fortitude by coming to terms with how—rather than why—he was feeling boxed in.

According to Natsume Soseki's novel, *The Three-Cornered World* (*Kusa Makura*),

- *There is no escape from this world.*

As in Jean-Paul Sartre's play, there is *No Exit*. There is no artificial or arbitrary cushion to soften the impact of a negative feeling. This Zen saying captures the experience of facing harsh reality for what it is, "You can't move forward, you can't turn back, and you can't stand still. Where do you go?" The bottoming out of distress and despair that allows you to learn the necessary lessons and rebound from the depths of the abyss is known as:

- *Banging your head against a stone pillar*; or
  Taking a chisel and jabbing yourself over and over.

Accepting reality for what it is, the good and the bad with all the warts and imperfections, leads you to take full responsibility for your actions. According to the injunction of Smokey the Bear,

- *Only YOU can prevent forest fires!*

In an old aftershave commercial, a man with a tough beard gets slapped in the face with the lotion and responds, "Thanks. I needed that!" In order to rebound from suffering and discover the Buddha within and without one must reconcile with and accept frustration as a fundamental condition of existence.

We are used to thinking of advance and decline not in terms of self-development, but of external standards and procedures, rules and regulations, conventions and appearances. When these resources fall short or fail to deliver the expected results, rather than apportioning blame or relying on others, the best option for producing change is to turn within. This can generate momentum for projects and priorities, such as new funding sources, alternative collaborations, or diversified options for purchase or distribution.

Confronted with surprise announcements, ordinary doubt leaves your head spinning. You find yourself swimming in a sea of rumors, impressions, speculation, hearsay, wish lists, and pipe dreams, with a bit of innuendo tossed in. There is nothing to be gained from looking back or playing the blame game. It doesn't help to ask the boss directly, in a way that may seem challenging, threatening, or intimidating, when or why the promotion got delayed or at what point the decision to hand over the assignment was made. Brooding over the past will not unlock the complexity of what really happened, and will probably not yield useful information. Trying to discover the specific cause for your disappointment by logical thinking quickly reaches a dead end. Instead, consider from the standpoint of intuition what can now be done.

Shikata ga nai! is a Japanese saying that literally means "there's nothing you can do about it." As John Hersey describes in *Hiroshima*, this idiom became a touchstone for many of the survivors dealing with the aftermath of radiation sickness. Shikata ga nai! can imply throwing up your hands in disgusted defeat, as in "you can't fight City Hall," but it can also express a creative resignation that accepts what cannot be changed while refusing to capitulate to what can still be corrected. According to Zen, following the coldest winter snow comes the flowering of early spring blossoms.

Getting lost in the "coulda', woulda', shoulda'" syndrome ends in ignoring or denying what actually exists. A *Peanuts* comic strip offers a humorous illustration of the futility of indulging in misguided protest. Charlie Brown offers, "Some people would rather light a candle than curse the darkness," but in the last frame there is Lucy standing outside in the middle of the night screaming, "You stupid darkness!" When you reach the median between acceptance, or not resisting what cannot be changed, and nonacceptance, which continually presses for reform, you realize that,

• *The greater the doubt, the greater the enlightenment.*

Tryin' to Get to Heaven

Although Zen speaks of an "instant of awakening," it is not something that happens quickly as measured by the ticking of a clock. It is not really a point in time, but the "all of a sudden" quality that occurs at the completion of a longstanding process of development. According to the anonymous author of the medieval Christian mystical text known as *The Cloud of Unknowing*,

• *In one tiny moment, heaven may be gained or lost.*

Sometimes what you know is bound to change at any moment never does, forcing you to adjust your thinking. On other occasions, out of nowhere, an exciting possibility or a terrifying danger emerges with clarity and forcefulness. At any moment a difficult situation can be turned into a winning opportunity, yet it only takes the blink of an eye for a great opportunity to vanish into thin air, or what you thought was a triumph dissolves into just another idle speculation and unfulfilled expectation. Perhaps the sense that something significant seems on the way evaporates in the cold light of objective reality.

Telling the victories from the defeats is challenging as they get intertwined in trade-offs, compromises, and partial perspectives. It all goes by so fast. Either we tend to stop and think about how to react, suffering from the hesitation blues, or we rush in like fools and respond without thinking at all. This is not just the hectic pace of modern industrialized society.

Ordinarily, we perceive time as a natural force that carries us along inexorably like a river in flood. St. Augustine points out,

• *Time takes no holiday.*

On the other hand, the Hatter in *Alice's Adventures in Wonderland*, who occupies a realm where time seems to be standing still, says that the problem for most people is that they think of time as something impersonal and suggests somewhat paradoxically that you should not "talk about wasting *it*. It's *him*."

According to an advertising slogan, "Man invented time and Seiko perfected it." Augustine, who said that if he wasn't asked about time he understood it, but when asked he could not fathom it—that is, it's far easier to tell the time than to tell what time is—shows that the slogan is misleading. What man invented and Seiko perfected is timekeeping, not time. Man did not create time. The solar, lunar, and seasonal cycles all occur whether or not man even exists. Therefore, the slogan could be written to say,

- *God created time, and it is up to man to perfect it.*

Zen teaches that heaven can be gained through a sudden flash of insight referred to by the Japanese term **Satori.** Triggered by an insignificant comment or observation, an intense instant of inspiration hits home like a ton of bricks. You shed attachments and distractions as the clouds of ignorance disperse and the light of day shines through, revealing a clear view of the mountain peak. Anecdotes about Zen masters who attain enlightenment through the sudden path describe a variety of seemingly ordinary experiences: hearing the sound of a bamboo stick striking an object; seeing the petals of a flower open up or begin to fall; listening to the song of a bird or the thunder of a waterfall. Satori may also come from observing a teacher's enigmatic gesture, such as smiling silently while holding up a flower, turning on a lamp in the middle of the night, or lighting a fire in broad daylight.

Instead of regretting the past or fearing the future and letting the ticking clock become a tyrant, you discover ways to master time by regulating the perception of flux. Understanding time should be based on experiencing the full **Moment** of activity in the present. An oft-cited Zen saying about the essence of spiritual realization simply affirms,

- *When hungry I eat, when tired I sleep.*

According to traditional masters, living without disturbance means you must not neglect your current chosen task, whatever it may be, so that if it is hard to fall asleep you do not compensate by eating. When eating, perform that function only (and do not let your mind wander or get caught up in worry), and when sleeping do that and only that (and do not let agitation keep you awake).

The wrong approach is portrayed in one of the most famous koans, which could be dubbed the parable of "The Eager Monk." A novice who cannot wait to achieve enlightenment comes to the monastery to train with the master, but is turned away by the guard. He stays outside in the rain, sitting in zazen, until the gatekeeper finally grants him entrance. Once inside, he confronts an impasse at each step as he tries to fit into the monastic system. But this only makes him more eager and determined to attain his goal without delay. If only he could get an interview with Chao-chou, the master of the temple, he thinks his problems would be solved.

Early one morning, he finally gains permission to meet the great teacher, a rare privilege for a novice in the highly stratified monastic hierarchy. Chao-chou senses that he has an "eager beaver" on his hands. He asks the young monk if he has taken his morning meal (which in the monastery consists of rice gruel). When the novice answers, "Yes, of course," Chao-chou instructs him,

- *Go back and wash the breakfast bowls.*

The monk is dismissed and the meeting ends abruptly. Chao-chou tells the eager monk that he needs to be more humble and more patient, and that the quest for enlightenment must happen in a sequential fashion. You can't bypass the next logical step in the path by trying to leap ahead before you are prepared.

In some cases, it seems that heaven is won and lost at the very same time. Positive and negative elements are so entangled that it may be impossible to distinguish them, for they strengthen as well as diminish one another. In an episode of the old *Superman* TV show, Jimmy Olsen and Lois Lane stumble onto a cache of stolen money. But then they get stuck in the attic of a house with a suitcase full of hundred dollar bills and no way out of the predicament, except to burn the money in a fireplace to send a smoke signal to Superman.

Urged on by Lois, Jimmy reluctantly consigns every last bill to the flames to ensure a strong signal. At the height of the fantasy about what could be gained, circumstances shifted and the position of strength was undercut. The question turned in an instant from, "What can I do with what I will acquire?" to "How can I make the most of what I have before it is gone?" Just as the heaven of rescue and safety is won the goal of gaining fame and fortune is lost.

When I was a kid, my favorite sports team was the football squad at the college where my father and other family members had gone to school. We would go out to the games nearly every weekend. However, my team was in lousy shape. Just a few years before they had been a real powerhouse, but then the school joined a new conference that placed a policy of de-emphasis on sports development. The team was stuck playing nationally ranked rivals without summer training camp or high-level recruiting and lost every game for three seasons straight. Then, the very next year, the coach who had lived through the humiliation finally found himself playing more evenly matched teams on the schedule and was on the verge of winning the league championship.

I went to the final game of the year one brilliant Saturday afternoon, and I still remember how the star quarterback threw four touchdown passes that day and the defense shut out the opponents. The final score was 28–0, and we were champions. For that day of joy in Mudville, my excitement knew no bounds. The next morning I opened the sports section of the Sunday paper and expected to read all about it. Instead, the big story was that the coach was fired. In fact, he had been informed just before kickoff, and probably the quarterback knew this during the game.

When I asked my father how this could possibly be the case, he made a comment about the right hand of an institution often not knowing what the left hand is doing. Thinking about this more carefully, I wondered if maybe the irony had occurred precisely because the two hands did know what the other was up to. Which way was it? This question became the conundrum I have grappled with for many a moon, a personal puzzle, my koan.

In a determinative moment, winning and losing, heaven and hell, are never distinct, separate, either/or possibilities, but often represent states of mind that are interwoven at every level. There is a Zen saying that a monk who gained a realization, while being outsmarted by a rival master, "came back to life while in the midst of death." In a single instant, truth may be discovered in the midst of untruth. The error of your ways may lead you on the right path, but it can also happen that when you feel bound to reach a goal there is a fatal misstep at the eleventh hour.

Japanese poets eulogize the falling cherry blossoms because they evoke the fleeting, uncertain nature of existence.

• *Parting is such sweet sorrow.*

As Shakespeare knew, joy is tinged with poignant sadness, and sorrow has its sweetness. Even tragedy may bear a silver lining from which new optimism springs forth. The fragility of life revealed in a single moment can contain at once exhilaration and regret.

Wallpaper Satori

Senpai once felt a Shakespearean moment when troubling circumstances led him to a realization of the powerful role of the Unmoving Mind. He was often asked to lead workshops for students and trainees on creative approaches to acquire funding, including gaining financial support from a government agency or foundation.

Usually Senpai began the workshop by recalling that years ago he was a novice attending the same kind of activity during a deep economic recession. Hard times meant that the participants in the training were many and varied. There were a number of people whose careers had been cut off in midstream by cutbacks and restructuring, and who now sought to retool their skills. Many other participants were weighing options and contemplating possibilities or fallback plans that they would never have had to think about in fatter times.

In considering these worst-case scenarios, everyone in the room was probably thinking that it might be necessary to throw away years of preparation, planning, and dreaming. In the harsh light of reality, you are forced to consider drastic, dramatic change by assessing possibilities rather than desires and analyzing exactly what your skills are and might become as opposed to what your credentials and interests have been. What abilities have you developed, irrespective of context or substance, that could possibly be refashioned and applied to a whole new type of pursuit? Writing and wordprocessing skills may be rerouted into technical editing or journalism. Knowledge of history or world cultures could be useful in working for a museum, a travel agency, or consulting for international marketing or management firms.

Faced with the prospect of finding imaginative ways to enhance or revamp their existing skills, the workshop participants seemed gripped with anxiety. As the team leader went around the room for the usual self-introductions, Senpai felt as if he had landed in a group therapy session. Some were eager to pour out their tales of woe and bare their souls to the entire group. The atmosphere in the room became tense with expectation as they waited for the last of the featured speakers, a famed consultant renowned for his ability to navigate the highways and byways of agency funding.

Senpai fell to thinking that here he was in a room full of Ronin, or leaderless samurai, who were all looking for a structure, a framework, or bedrock of support to lean on. The goal of major grant funding had slipped through his fingers just three weeks before when he was told that his proposal had been rejected. Looking back at all the negotiations and deals brokered that had put him in a position to submit a competitive proposal, he tried to find a Zen Mind amid his misfortunes.

Sitting in the workshop, Senpai realized that time was getting short when the consultant finally arrived. The room was overtaken by a hush. From the outset, the speaker was extremely knowledgeable and offered all kinds of valuable suggestions and helpful tips. But his offhand manner seemed overly casual to many. The more emotional the participants, the more independent he appeared, and this increased their agitation.

The consultant's lack of engagement was obviously becoming a source of frustration for one particularly vocal member of the group. She felt she was already very familiar with the options being discussed, and she started to exhibit a chip on the shoulder, "What else can you show me?" attitude. The others appreciated the healthy dose of skepticism injected by her line of questioning. But they also became uneasy as the eagerly anticipated chance to benefit from the workshop was rapidly slipping away.

Then the skeptical participant stood up and announced that she had gone through rounds of rejection from some of the same agencies the consultant was recommending as good prospects. She wanted to know how his recommendations would lead her to a positive result this time. She finally blurted out,

- *Why should I waste my time following your suggestions? Haven't I received enough rejections already?*

The speaker sat back in his chair, unfazed and unflustered. With a calm indifference reflecting years of experience and many rounds of successes and failures, he replied,

- *I would not feel alone in this. Everybody gets rejection slips. I could paper my walls with rejection slips.*

With a wry grin, he picked up a piece of paper that might have been one of the famed rejection slips, and ceremoniously crumpled it up and threw it in Senpai's direction. For Senpai, this remark and gesture, as well as the speaker's knowing glance towards him produced a genuine flash of insight. He did not remember what else was said that day. Everything else seemed irrelevant, as did the question asked on the evaluation form about whether the speaker had done his job well in light of the participants' expectations.

What was powerful about the speaker was evidence of an Unmoving Mind that showed a caring kind of indifference, beyond doubting—or maybe it was an indifferent form of compassion. Yukio Mishima, who was quite critical of the role of Zen in modern Japan, nevertheless depicted an authentic Zen master in his novel, *Temple of the Golden Pavilion*:

- *There was a gentleness in his thundering voice that found an echo in my heart. It was not a usual sort of gentleness, but the gentleness of the harsh roots of some great tree that grows outside a village and gives shelter to the passing traveler.*

The speaker had shown anti-structure in action. His answer was a bold stroke that broke out of the box. There was apparent harshness, but it was clear this did not reveal lack of concern or consideration towards the questioner or the other participants. Rather, his response embodied a typical Zen paradox, that in order to show that you really care you have to show that you do not care. This was exactly the lesson they needed to learn in their search for jobs and funding—to have the confidence and Sansom strength that demonstrates to prospective employers or supervisors that you are not desperate and, in fact, can walk away from any situation. This kind of indifference approach does not reflect stubbornness or a maverick mentality but a degree of resolve that may not be contained within ordinary structure.

For Senpai, the stress of being constrained in his professional choices had been lifted. He could again straighten his shoulders and shake off that debilitating anxiety. Leaving the workshop, Senpai had gained a tremendous resolve to pursue his goals and

muster whatever he could to be successful. The alienation of being a Ronin turned out to be a growing experience for Senpai
because it provided an opportunity to stand outside every system in order to be that much more productive once he found his
way back inside.

A few months later, after repeatedly checking and inquiring,
he received notification that a fellowship candidacy, which had
been stalled on a waiting list, was accepted. Another good prospect also opened up as a fallback. The fellowship led to a couple
of years of research in the field, which was clearly the greatest
turning point in his career path, and Plan B also eventually came
through with very productive results. Winning the fellowship was
the result of active self-direction, and the fallback plan reflected a
purposeful use of doubt. By realizing that the potential to man-
age future advancement as well as to encounter disappointment
were both harbored within, Senpai was able to keep momentum
going during difficult times.

In Western religion, a spontaneous breakthrough to a new level
of understanding that is triggered by a seemingly minor event is
known as an epiphany. A Satori or epiphany usually comes when
you have been struggling to solve a problem without budging past
the initial impasse. Then, when you are just at the point of giving
up hope, the answer suddenly becomes obvious. This is not the
same as a quick and impulsive idea, or a mere surprise. Instead, it
reflects an ongoing process of building and developing that creates the opportunity for insight.

The flash of insight invariably feels unexpected and unsought.
According to a Zen saying,

- *Do not engage in useless seeking. Only when you have nothing
  in your mind and are vacant and open to the spiritual mystery
  will you discover the marvelous nature of true reality.*

Satori occurs in an instant but is the fruition of a long-term development. You are like a cup that is filled to the brim. What does

it take to make it overflow? The addition of just a single drop of water.

A weight comes off your shoulders and the burden of anxiety is removed when you gain clarity about a problem you have been struggling with. Frustration and futility fade like the morning dew as you no longer feel lost or trapped by circumstance, but can act decisively to seize a ripe opportunity. The fleeting yet life-altering insight sparked by a casual, offhand comment leads to a renewed sense of resolve, as in Bob Dylan's words,

> *Casting off one more layer of skin,*
> *Keeping one step ahead of the persecutor within.*

Bill Evans, a pianist in the late 1950s, compared improvisational jazz to Zen. His liner notes for the album *Kind of Blue* performed by the Miles Davis sextet (including Evans as well as John Coltrane on sax) capture the relation between improvisation (or anti-structure) and the continuity of form (or structure) needed to make the momentary experience endure:

- *There is a Japanese visual art in which the artist is forced to be spontaneous. He must paint on a thin-stretched parchment with a special brush and black water paint in such a way that an unnatural or interrupted stroke will destroy the line or break through the parchment. Erasures or changes are impossible. These artists must practice in a particular discipline, that of allowing the idea to express itself in communication with their hands in such a direct way that deliberation cannot interfere.*

The discipline of practice and the understanding of the formal properties of the composition free the jazz musician to improvise in an effective and spontaneous fashion. In much the same way, cultivating the Unmoving Mind enables its possessor to react to events as they occur around her. Jazz, like Zen, does not have room for second thoughts or items left on the cutting room floor, so to speak, and it manifests the "conviction that direct deed is the most meaningful reflection," according to Evans.

Zen teaches us not to let the moment pass. As the ancient Jewish philosopher Hillel similarly asked,

- *If not now, when?*

The experience of the Moment, which encompasses the past through memory and recollection and reaches into the future in anticipation, stills anxieties. Standing rooted in "now" means being open and ready for "then" to weigh your strengths and weaknesses, potential and constraints for growth, and to gauge how these can be balanced in the appropriate way. You may want to try to cut your losses by responding swiftly and appropriately or to remain patient despite odds and obstacles.

Suppose a problem of limited resources in funding, personnel, or equipment—a budget cut, a co-worker who takes another job, or a broken computer—is revealed today—and you foresee that the problem is likely to get worse, whether in two months or two years. On the one hand, you do not want to get ahead of yourself and become preoccupied with this contingency to the detriment of your focus on current activities. But you also realize you must begin planning right now, handling all your affairs in a way that either offsets potential problems or puts fallback strategies in motion.

You need to develop a **Long View** that looks ahead to scenarios that will play out over days, weeks, months, or years, but without sacrificing concentration now. This is expressed in a line from the Mel Brooks movie, *The Twelve Chairs*:

- *Hope for the best, expect the worst. Life is a play. We are unrehearsed.*

CHAPTER FIVE

Seeing the Forest,
But Not Missing the Trees

Four Levels of Consciousness

I N CONSTRUCTING AN EVALUATION of his rival's project, Senpai realized that the rebuilding of character is not something simply to be thought about. It must be demonstrated through appropriate speech. How you get your message across determines the balance between gaining and losing heaven in that tiny moment.

As suggested by the opening of Soscki's novel, *The Three Cornered World*, people often find themselves tied up in knots and have difficulty expressing their attitudes and aims because they cannot properly coordinate the various cognitive elements involved in persuasive communication. Their speech is misguided when being produced under the sway of ordinary feelings or thoughts that are choked by the tenacious weeds of assumptions and presumptions:

- *Approach everything rationally, and you become harsh. Pole along in the stream of emotions, and you will be swept away by the current. Give free rein to your desires, and you become uncomfortably confined. It is not a very agreeable place to live, this world of ours.*

For Soseki, feelings and desire offer only the illusion of freedom, but reason does not necessarily provide the answer. It can become just another constraint that keeps you rigid and inflexible, and thus still not in control of your reactions.

In a later passage, Soseki proposes a solution to the communication impasse by means of which you can,

- *Enter at will a world of undefiled purity, and throwing off the yoke of avarice and self interest, are able to build up a peerless and unequaled universe.*

The transition from self-interest to self-control hinges on cultivating through EPA the four basic levels of consciousness. The first level is **feeling** or emotion, which includes your immediate gut responses to people or events. Getting foxed hits home here, producing dismay and dejection. This is the realm where external stimuli affect you first, for better or worse, but you can elevate and transform emotions by achieving a depersonalized perspective.

The second level is **speaking**, which can be calm and constructive if guided by higher states of consciousness, or it can be driven by emotions in a way that increases conflict. This level of consciousness encompasses style as well as content. Speaking does not refer only to the act of uttering words, but the state of mind in giving voice or expression to feelings and ideas. The way you communicate is a crucial factor in whether, in the end, you are able to make your case.

The next level is **thinking**, or rational, logical calculation. Reason provides a careful systematic analysis by offering a check-and-balance that prevents feelings from getting out of control or being expressed as an extreme form of reaction.

Unless freed of bias stemming from emotions, thinking will produce a distorted analysis and in turn taint speaking, revealing the anxiety associated with uncertain or unstable conclusions. But when empowered by logic that enables a careful, objective examination, thinking keeps emotions in line and allows your speech to be eloquent and convincing. However, speaking based solely on rationality may come across as rigid and not very compelling. Thinking, as the third level of consciousness, can be one-dimensional if you are locked into a pattern of either/or, yes-or-no conceptualization, and do not take advantage of the fuller range of options.

Therefore, logic is not the highest level, according to Zen. An analytic mode of thought may be inadequate when faced with a crisis or conflict involving interpersonal relations and complex negotiations. Such times demand not only a rational examination of the external world, but a deep internal, subjective understanding in order to result in decisive action.

For example, when denied a bonus, raise, or promotion, your gut reaction is to question the decision. If you express your frustration histrionically, a supervisor will likely simply turn you away. A more measured and objective tone indicates that you have thought things through and are prepared to accept the outcome. However, in relying on logic alone, you may have an understanding that does not have the power to change the results. At this point, the capacities of the first three levels of consciousness run into a dead end and you may find yourself blindsided by an even more unexpected or daunting distraction. A Zen koan instructs,

- *It is not a matter of thinking, which is too analytic, or of not-thinking, which is a blank state of consciousness. How do you think beyond thinking?*

What is missing is a lofty wisdom or sense of balance that synthesizes and moderates emotion and reason to adjust agendas in response to the perpetually shifting tide of circumstances. The Greek term for "word" is *logos*, which is the root of "logic" in modern English. In ancient Greek, *logos* had less to do with actual speaking than the collecting of thoughts behind the words and it implied "light" in the sense of the source of inspiration.

The fourth level, **knowing** or intuitive awareness, is essential for integrating the other states. It is the cohesive or binding factor that enables the entire process of communication to function smoothly. Intuition sharpens but is not bound by the rules of logic, so that it is sometimes referred to as "unknowing" in Christian mysticism, just as the Mind is often called No-Mind by some Zen masters. The importance of opening up intuition is understood in many mystical traditions, but Zen specializes in refining its capacities while diminishing its perils. Intuitive awareness allows you to act-and-react spontaneously, which is crucial for making the transition from structure to anti-structure that can turn a conflictive Confrontation into a productive Encounter.

The fourth level is a state of being or way of acting. Whereas thinking analyzes the prior cause and subsequent effect of any event, knowing understands reality in terms of interrelated roots and branches unfolding simultaneously. This insight enables you to summon strength of character and demonstrate in a creative and resourceful way that you deserve to achieve your goals. Picture yourself at a crossroads, whether an actual intersection or a metaphorical one, such as a choice of career. The term Tao in Chinese, which literally denotes road, originally meant "way making" or carving out a route. At a time when there were few human-made thoroughfares you had to find your own way through the wilderness on each and every journey. Eventually you came to recognize landmarks and signs left by you as well as other passersby and a new, more long-lasting path was created.

Choices made at a juncture are never based simply on binary oppositions like stop or go, slow down or speed up, turn left or turn right. For one thing, several of these decisions can be made simultaneously and may complement or contradict one another. New elements arise and others' reactions influence your perceptions or cause ideas to dawn. There are so many fluctuating opportunities and obstacles that you vacillate between logic and instinct. Each time a decision is being made, logical analysis dissects alternatives into patterns of dichotomy and expansive intuitive awareness tries to steer instinctively towards the overriding goals or targets of operation.

Switching from the level of thinking to intuition often happens when you are in jeopardy or walking a tightrope and need to make a leap of faith. I learned this lesson during my first trip to Japan. I was going to attend a conference in an out-of-the-way neighborhood in Tokyo. Tokyo is a very confusing place to try to get around. Not only is it a vast and labyrinthine metropolis, but also the system of street addresses is rooted in a medieval technique for deceiving would-be attackers. The custom for locals and outsiders alike is to ask directions from a police officer, who is likely to draw you a map.

When I got off at the subway station and realized I was running late, I saw a tall Westerner emerge from the crowd. I knew that the conference was going to draw both foreign and Japanese researchers and that a prominent professor from the United States would be the keynote speaker. I had never seen the professor before but something inside me said that following this gentleman would lead me safely to shore. In a split second, I had to decide whether to quickly pursue the bobbing figure as it was disappearing in a sea of bodies ascending the stairs to ground level or look for a police station where I would ask for directions in Japanese. The second option would be a little tedious and time consuming but more likely to yield accurate results. Of course, I instinctively trailed behind the foreigner and sure enough, he was the keynote speaker.

Reacting based on feelings could have led me to panic, but I did not have the time to sit back and think it through rationally. Instead, I relied on knowing, which is a self-regulating mechanism that synthesizes the other levels of consciousness while maintaining a focus on the ultimate purpose of any project. The fourth level prevents feelings from being violent or indifferent, keeps speaking from revealing hostility or declining into idle chatter, and cuts off thinking from being led around by the arbitrary rules of reason as if these were the rulers of Self.

There are three main aspects of the four levels of consciousness. The first aspect is that these elements of human behavior have an innate functional unity as indicated in the following diagram.

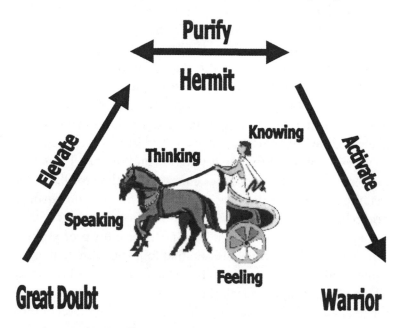

Feeling is like the wheels of a chariot, which constantly comes in contact with the outside world. Speaking is the horses, which propel us forward, and thinking is the reins that guide the horses. But it is the charioteer, who is continually making decisions about speed and direction by keeping in Mind the goal of reaching the final destination, who controls all these factors.

The second aspect is that each of the levels is a two-edged sword. It can bring enhancement when aligned and balanced through contemplation and concentration following the Great Doubt. When untamed and separate from the other levels, however, it can be a destructive force by manipulating circumstances.

According to Buddhist teaching, an imbalance arises in the first three levels of consciousness when feelings respond reflexively to external stimulation and immediately become entangled in self-interested motives and intentions. Caught up in the desire for what is absent or revulsion at what is present, feelings easily lead to an "us-versus-them" mentality. Emotions are polarized into a fundamental opposition between liking or trying to acquire more and more of what feels pleasant and disliking or trying to eliminate more and more of what feels unpleasant. Acting on these unconscious impulses can become locked into a fixed pattern of behavior so deeply ingrained that it seems impossible to break out of it.

According to many accounts in social psychology, which lend support to Buddhist teachings, employers make up their minds about job candidates almost at first sight. Once the initial impression has registered, it is nearly irreversible. In the case of the unwanted assignment, for example, you are being evaluated from the moment the supervisor walks through the door. An instant of delay may create an impression that will work against you for some time to come.

The Unmoving Mind develops as you are able to restructure an initial instant of perception—that tiny moment—so that in your first impressions you do not make judgments instinctively, giving rise to polarization, but rather remain open and objective. Instead of saying to yourself, "I like this and want more of it" or "I do not like this and want less," you remain calm and composed.

Speaking stands in a middle ground between feelings and thoughts. When driven by excessive emotions and inner turmoil, words express aggression and promote disharmony. An overly emotional speech provoked by a feeling of powerlessness can earn one a reputation as temperamental and capricious, a label that may be tough able to shake. If balanced and in harmony with the other levels of consciousness, speaking is a constructive means of persuasion that makes effective use of multiple factors such as tone and diction that affect the impact of communication. On the other hand, the aligned state of this level of consciousness can also yield an overreliance on discourse at the expense of following through. Actions speak louder.

Part of constructive communication is to depersonalize both criticism and praise. Rather than referring to a particular person informally as John, which may indicate disrespect, or formally as Mr. Brown, which seems stilted, refer to his role: "The director has indicated such and such," is enunciated either to distance from the function of criticism or to evoke the power of authority. Taking the progression a step further means referring not to the person or the position but to the office, as in the "management office has announced …" The path of neutrality refrains from making mountains out of molehills or vice versa, because mountains are mountains and molehills are molehills. Of course, this technique can be misused as a way of treating colleagues with less of a sense of individuality and integrity than is deserved.

Knowing can deteriorate into partiality and one-sidedness if it is guided by unproductive or even destructive emotions that have not been fully extirpated. Senpai once knew a visionary colleague who had ideas sprouting all over the place but difficulty in translating them into action because he didn't understand the importance of engaging others in the necessary planning. He was seduced by the thrill of the kill in chasing down the concept or contact, not realizing that an idea expressed at the wrong time, however illuminating, can easily backfire if full support is not in place to make things happen. The colleague had particular difficulty in coordinating external resources with internal support. One time he had obtained outside backing for a plan but was flummoxed when told that there was nothing to sustain it on the inside. Another time, insiders were attracted to a project he envisioned but when he could not deliver the external factors, it was said that instead of lining up his ducks he had taken out a shotgun and fired at them.

Levels	Unaligned	Aligned
Knowing (Intuition)	Partial	Boundless
Thinking (Logic)	Manipulative	Objective
Speaking (Communication)	Attacking	Persuasive
Feeling (Emotion)	Polarized	Depersonalized

The third aspect of the four levels of consciousness is that the Moment of convergence of intuition and logic, or unconscious impulse and conscious striving, is the Satori's instantaneous flash of insight. It is the light bulb going on or a lightning bolt from the blue, the lifting of the veil to reveal a realm of clarity.

Senpai experienced the positive side of intuition when he was being reviewed for a competition to earn an important credential. He had to go through a series of oral exams, each conducted by a different interviewer. He felt he was doing well until he got to the final interview of the day and the reviewer pressed him on theoretical issues despite the fact that his expertise was in applications. The first two questions were so perplexing that Senpai evoked an obscure rule that allowed you to turn away three queries. He knew that even though one more pass was technically permissible, it might well sink his chances. So he leapt into the discussion, showing the interviewer a way to refashion the second question so that in the process he could pull out what he knew rather than expose what he did not. He passed the test.

Learning Unlearning

The ability to respond immediately to complex situations means that you can free yourself from preconceptions and **unlearn** counterproductive habits, such as building up demands and expectations.

Through the insight of the Hermit, who believes each person is a Buddha waiting to be discovered, feelings are tamed and cleared of attachments and negativity, and this enables persuasive communication. The Zen path was greatly influenced by the philosophy of Lao Tzu, the founder of Taoism, who suggests,

- *To succeed in the world you must learn more and more,*
  But to accomplish in the realm of the Tao you must
  unlearn.

Chuang Tzu, another early Taoist thinker whose writings influenced Zen, talked about the path of "forgetting" or casting aside self-defeating habits along with the weeds of mundane attachments.

This stage is followed by a "fasting of the mind," which blocks the influx of contaminating thoughts in order to maintain a state of nimbleness and agility. Just as the body does not partake of food after the midday meal in traditional Buddhist monasticism or during holy days such as Yom Kippur, Lent, or Ramadan in other religions, so the mind refrains from the intake of pollutants. Yet, according to a biblical passage (Matthew 15:11), ingestion is not the main issue:

- *It is not what goes into your mouth that defiles a person, but it is what comes out of the mouth that defiles.*

In many religious traditions, a celebratory feast follows a fast marking repentance. In Taoist mysticism, spiritual feasting is known as the path of "free and easy wandering," which explores all perspectives without fixation:

- *Learn and unlearn*
  Learn to unlearn, for
  To unlearn is to learn.

Unlearning to be preoccupied with the polarities of winning and losing enables you to look carefully at other points of view.

You analyze each person and situation on a case-by-case basis to determine what you know for sure and what you do not know and are only guessing or conjecturing. As Confucius says,

- *Knowledge means when you know a thing to recognize that you know it, and when you do not know a thing to recognize that you do not know it. That is knowledge.*

Detective Joe Friday on the old *Dragnet* TV series cautioned witnesses not to offer hearsay, guesswork, rumor, or innuendo,

- *Just the facts, Ma'am.*

Any hint of favoritism may be detrimental to a reputation for good judgment, as well as the ability to recommend reforms. Physicist Julian Barbour says of the greatest of modern scientists, who "have deep-rooted but false ideas about the nature of space, time, and things,"

- *Preconceptions obscure the true nature of the world.*

What is needed is the attitude of Galileo, who in debating with those who exhibited a mulish adherence to Greek cosmology swore,

- *If Aristotle himself were brought back to life and shown the sights now seen, the great philosopher would quickly alter his opinion.*

In reaching a state of disinterested detachment, or what French thinkers call *desinteressement*, the Hermit realizes that, if taken to an extreme, every emotion without exception to the rule, no matter how worthy it seems in itself, will become problematic. Love becomes an obsession or joy turns into a preoccupation when these seemingly positive emotions become fixed on a single object. However, moderation as an end in itself is no better if it cuts off alternatives arbitrarily and prevents you from exploring and experiencing every possible vantage point. When integrated and harmonized with the higher levels, however, emotions become still and depersonalized, and no longer interfere. But the aligned or awakened aspect of feelings can also be problematic if it is too detached and creates the appearance of mere indifference or is uncritical in a way that leaves you vulnerable to getting foxed.

A painting depicts an ancient Chinese hermit escaping political intrigue by retreating to the countryside. In a state of **Dwelling on the Peak**, he dips his hand into a waterfall to wash his ears of the contaminated words he recently heard in the capital, reflecting a balanced perspective that perpetually rises above strife and discord.

In assessing his rival, for example, Senpai did not look back at the possible reasons why he lost the competition but stayed focused on the evaluation in front of him. Through the path of **Neutrality** (or openendedness) and **Equanimity** (or evenhandedness), the Hermit way overcomes the vicious cycle of seeking to acquire what is desired and eliminate what is undesired. Instead of reacting out of unbridled feeling, you step away from the scene, climb to the proverbial mountaintop of comprehensive awareness, and gain a bird's-eye view of the situation.

Neutrality is not a deadened state, withdrawn from engagement. The Hermit attains a unified vision that transcends yet at the same time stays actively involved in the realm of division and variation in the valley below. His speaking does not avoid conflict or competition but turns confrontational situations into avenues for constructive interaction. As a genuine middle path between the extremes of passivity and aggressiveness, neutrality is fully alive and aware of a boundless array of opportunities. Therefore,

- *Withdrawal (or silence) does not disable activity (or speaking), but ultimately empowers it.*

The Hermit way culminates in the comprehensive awareness that Taoism calls the "equality of all things," which is useful in solving dilemmas in the mundane realm where everything seems unequal and divisive. Picture a manager whose staff is ever complaining about the system of rewards. The manager offers those employees who achieve a high level of productivity four bonuses in the first quarter and three in the second quarter. The staff is not satisfied and threatens to rebel. The manager then reverses himself and offers three bonuses in the first quarter and four in the second. Now everyone is content. Nothing has changed. Reality stays the same and comes out in the end to the identical state; however, the new way of divvying up the rewards gives the workers a psychological boost.

The overseer tries to instruct the workers that understanding equality provides peace of mind. When you accept that opportunities are limited, you free yourself from the constraints of misleading expectations and demands. This insight gave Senpai a chance to stop counting his wins and losses on a spreadsheet, or calculating pluses and minuses as he gazed at the record of the rival. Instead he could focus on the process of evaluation, leaving personal goals (his or the rival's) of fame and fortune, or reputation and recognition to emerge, or not, as by-products rather than primary aims.

Imagine you are arguing with your spouse about which car to buy, domestic or foreign, SUV or van, sedan or wagon, bright color or dark color, automatic or manual. The debate quickly escalates into a feud that infiltrates every aspect of your relationship. In the midst of the most heated stage of the argument, you take the elevator to the top floor of a high rise. You look down and the cars below appear like tiny, featureless specks. At that moment, you can laugh at yourself for having succumbed to such a petty obsession and you and your partner quickly are able to come to terms.

Consider a turf battle over something like a specific item, such as a proposal, report, submission, or request. Stepping back to a position of lofty objectivity allows you clearly and unemotionally to survey the pros and cons of each and every person, item, or event in its appropriate proportionality. To paraphrase another Confucian proverb,

* *Do not treat what is significant as not significant or what is not significant as significant.*

Then you can filter proposals and make resolute yet flexible decisions acceptable to the respective parties.

Following the spiritual paradox that serving and humility are preferable to being served and boasting, Zen teaches that complete objectivity in examining other perspectives frees you for greater self-reflection and introspection. No matter what your personal feelings, you must be eminently fair and reasonable in your assessment of overall and individual strengths and weaknesses, needs and goals. Do not pigeonhole anyone exclusively as an ally or an adversary, but rather be aware of subtle shifts in attitudes and behavior.

Treating employees well encourages your employers to do the same, according to karmic law of "do unto others ..." If someone under your supervision is doing an outstanding job, let people know how much you value their contribution, which may help lift their performance to the next level. Should they receive an offer from another firm, be sure there is a solid counteroffer. While you stay vigilant for errors and lapses, your critique will be more credible if you are on record as being unbiased.

A Mountain by Any Other Name

EPA is completed by integrating the way of the Hermit, which awakens the intuitive awareness that purifies intentions by making all things equal, with the way of the Warrior, which activates and applies the first three levels of consciousness, now free of bias and open to possibilities in concrete activities of the everyday world. Despite their fundamental differences in outlook, the best of Hermit and Warrior ways combined inspires the steadiness and spontaneity needed to face off with a difficult challenge.

The Hermit represents the possibility of stepping back from complicated emotional reactions and removing ego to see things clearly from an elevated perspective. The Hermit's practice of withholding emotions is a discipline necessary to the outlook of the Warrior, who competes with utmost effort on the institutional "battlefield." The Hermit way by itself may lead to passivity and renunciation and end in withdrawal and capitulation. The Warrior way by itself may lead to cold-blooded and manipulative behavior that is also excessively self-sacrificing and end in conflict and confrontation.

To create an Encounter, the Hermit adopts techniques of the Warrior to come out of isolation and becomes alert and prepared for an interpersonal exchange. To be a great Warrior on the level of dynamic activity is to be a great Hermit on the level of calm contemplation, and vice versa. This integration maximizes the impact of words and deeds while reducing or eliminating risk. White Collar Zen seeks to balance the two approaches, so that productive results are obtained and the potential for extremes and excesses is lessened.

Taking the path of contemplative action, the Warrior, who hears the clashing of swords and armor and at times the cry of the agony of defeat and death, represents the fulfillment of the Hermit's re-entry into mainstream society. In the final illustration of the series of Zen illustrations, the **Ten Oxherding Pictures**, "Returning to the Marketplace," the herder goes beyond the abstract transcendence represented by the empty circle of the eighth picture.

A frequently cited proverb lays out three main stages in the development of Zen intuitive insight:

- *1. Before studying Zen,*
  mountains are mountains and rivers are rivers;

2. *While studying Zen,*
   mountains are no longer mountains and rivers are no
   longer rivers;

3. *After studying Zen,*
   mountains are mountains and rivers are rivers, again.

According to a traditional explanation, the first stage reflects the view of a child who smells a flower or sees its bright colors and feels profound admiration. But the child is not capable of objective examination or interpretation of the significance of the natural object. The child only has unexamined impressions mixed with what he or she has heard or been taught. The second stage is that of the scientist, who may lose sight of the big picture while investigating details, categorizing reality in terms of cause and effect, divisions and subdivisions. Relying on thinking or reason, the scientist looks too carefully at particulars and is blind to the overview. Yet sometimes the scientist has a flash of intuitive insight and cries out in Satori-like fashion,

- *Eureka!*

The third stage is that of the poet, whose integrative intuition synthesizes the first two standpoints while transcending their limitations. The poet's approach is at once analytic or objective, like the scientist, and experiential or subjective, like the child. The poet sounds identical to the child, but has attained a more profound level of understanding as a result of having passed through the stage of the scientist. Telling the differences between the first and second perception of mountains as mountains is a crucial Zen skill.

Consider the way inexperienced workers approach professional associations. A long way from mastering their role, junior colleagues may feel anxious and intimidated by their superiors. But to succeed you need always to be shooting for something higher because some day you will want to be able to fill the shoes of the

people of whom you ar
inner circle of leadership
superiors.

Senpai often told dis
nars and panels at majo
to be perceived as bein;
was a crucial qualifier,
ready participated in or
someone too scared or i
damental difference be
tains and seeing them a

In the second stage,
channels, such as propo
and next being elected
role where you are cou
judgment is respected
process, you can transc
you are willing to star
new blood. You are no
the role and can let go
process of growth, yo
Becoming a senior ad
your work is overlook

The final stage of th
and surpasses the first
examining, learning, a
that mountains are on
the choices that allow

- *Making mount*

PART THREE

Mountains Are Mountains Again: From Structure to Anti-Structure

If the president is fearless and the general is fearless, then the troops will also be fearless.

Shaquille O'Neal

CHAPTER SIX

Returning to the Marketplace

Turning Things Upside Down, Zigzag, and Topsy-Turvy

Y OU HAVE PROBABLY HEARD the following advice at times when you were being headstrong, stubborn, or provocative, even if your point was basically correct:

- *Be cautious. Choose your battles wisely.*

This means that you are only going to win a certain number of battles and you don't want to waste your energy by fighting for things that are of subsidiary importance. For example, if your colleagues are unenthusiastic about a project you would like to pursue, you should only push back hard if it is very important to you personally. Even if it might be a worthwhile project that would prove successful, if you insist on getting your way on all or most of these cases you may forfeit credibility and clout. Your colleagues should know that if you fight for a project there must be something special about it. Otherwise, remain unemotional (objective and neutral) in presentation, and wait for a time when you are able to coordinate style and substance to attain success.

The Zen version of this saying in the professional sphere is,

* *Create your Encounters!*

The path of neutrality and equanimity is critical to your ability to transform a situation of competition from a Confrontation, which is one-dimensional and static, to an Encounter, which is multifunctional and fluid. In a Confrontation, words do not ease tensions or produce the desired change. Instead, they cause a rigid structure to become even more inflexible. A Confrontation compounds the sense of futility and may lead to further conflict without creating a fallback system, whereas an Encounter is a creative form of negotiation with mutually beneficial consequences. As Heraclitus says of the use of interaction for positive results,

* *That which opposes produces a benefit.*

Encouraging colleagues in a constructive way and being prepared to acknowledge what you learn from them earns respect while uplifting competitors and unallied forces.

In their Encounter dialogues, Zen masters generally express a challenge to conventional authority, and a decisive moment determines who holds genuine power (as a Buddha) and who has little but pretense and fakery (as a Fox). The Japanese term for Encounter dialogue, **kien-mondo**, refers to an "auspicious, dynamic opportunity" (*kien*) for a special meeting between parties who are destined to contest yet cooperate in a "question-answer" (*mondo*) process or dialogue that leads to the discovery of truth. The term *kien* suggests that fate leads you to meetings with people that may appear to be coincidental but in the end prove meaningful and decisive. This stands in contrast to another Japanese term, *guzen*, which indicates accidental or arbitrary incidents that are not part of a pattern, as well as fatalist notions that leave no room for free will and personal choice.

The realization that just the right person or circumstance has crossed your path marks the experience of "good *en*." These can be competitors or challengers if, in the end, you learn or benefit from the interaction. The "*en*" of "*kien*" is a productive meeting point of necessity and chance. Encounter dialogue is a way of testing and contesting in a game of oneupmanship with no clear, final victor, since even those who are seemingly defeated also gain rewards.

The patterns and lessons of Zen dialogues are brilliantly illustrated by a koan known as "**Te-shan** Carrying His Bundle," which provides a paradigm for the accomplishment of professional leadership goals. (A complete translation with commentaries is included in the Appendix).

> Te-shan came to see Kuei-shan. He carried his bundle into the Dharma Hall. Then he crossed from east side to west side, and again from west side to east side. He looked around and said, "No one is here. There's nothing here," and then he left.
>
> But when Te-shan got to the gates of the temple he thought to himself, "I really should not be so crude." So he entered the Dharma Hall once again, with full ceremony, to greet the master. Kuei-shan just sat there. Te-shan held up his training mat and said, "Teacher." Kuei-shan reached for his fly-whisk. Te-shan cried out, shook his sleeves, and abruptly left. Te-shan turned from the Dharma Hall, put on his straw sandals, and departed.
>
> That evening Kuei-shan asked the monk in charge of the Monks Hall, "Where is the newcomer who was with me earlier today?" The head monk said, "At that time he turned away from the Dharma Hall, put on his straw sandals, and departed." Kuei-shan said, "After this he will dwell on the summit of a peak all by himself, and build a hut where he scolds the Buddhas and reviles the Patriarchs."

The koan tells the story of an impromptu meeting of two masters. A young, aspiring monk walks unannounced into the central temple building, the Dharma Hall, and challenges an established

master, Kuei-shan, who was known for kicking over a water pitcher
to win the right to start his own monastery in the koan discussed
previously in chapter two. After meeting with Te-shan, Kuei-shan
at once claims victory and acknowledges defeat. Which of the two
masters has the Unmoving Mind? Who is the one whose mind is
easily swayed? In their exchange, which seems like a contest between Beat Zen or anti-structure (represented by Te-shan) and
Square Zen or structure (Kuei-shan), much is left ambiguous and
mysterious. No clear winner emerges, or more likely, both are victorious and enhanced through the competition.

The story begins with Te-shan arriving at the temple unexpected and disturbing Kuei-shan's claim to authority. "Carrying
his bundle" means that Te-shan arrives with a case full of sutras
(or scriptures) on his back, since he was known as "King of the
Sutras," along with such things as a begging bowl and healing
herbs. It also conveys the contemporary idea of carrying "baggage" in the sense of being weighed down by counterproductive
attitudes and anxieties. There are times when you need to check
your baggage at the entranceway and be open to a fresh experience, but it is clear from the outset that Te-shan is unable or un-
willing to do this. His strategy is to carry his portfolio, as a symbol
of his independence, straight into the corridors of power.

The **Dharma Hall** is the main building in the compound of
traditional Zen temples. In other forms of Buddhism, the most
important facility is the Buddha Hall, which houses statues as
objects of worship. Because Zen believes that the temple abbot is
a "living Buddha" and there is no need for traditional devotion, it
substituted the Dharma Hall for the Buddha Hall as the main
chamber of the compound. This is where the master sits on his
thronelike high seat and holds forth with a daily round of ser-
mons. Te-shan seems to come from nowhere and is at first able to
assert power by walking around. By going directly into the main
hall and skipping formalities, Te-shan makes a bold statement
that he is superior and not bound by the rules and routine of the

monastic institutional structure. He proclaims victory in saying, "No one is here"—in other words, "I win!"

With that overtly anti-structural approach, Te-shan is likely to get his comeuppance. A commentary on the koan describes him with a double insult,

- *Nothing but a wild fox spirit carrying a board across his shoulder.*

The commentator says that having the power of Zen does Te-shan little good. He comes off as arrogant, letting individuality get the best of him while neglecting the most basic display of manners in a formal ritual setting.

Te-shan's initial venture into anti-structure does not work because it comes too soon. It has not been set up properly. When earlier in his career Kuei-shan kicked over the water pitcher, he was successful in declaring his independence and integrity. His action was more effective than submitting to customs of protocol because it was not based on ego but rather was designed to express a deeper and more comprehensive understanding than his rival (who also tried but did not succeed at doing something anti-structural). The fact that Kuei-shan was awarded the establishment of his own monastery was the by-product rather than the purpose of his actions. Te-shan, however, merely appears disrespectful. He needs to go back to basics and follow proper channels before breaking out of them.

Te-shan realizes that he has been "too crude," a common insult in Zen dialogues, and must return to the Dharma Hall. His self-proclaimed victory is hollow without a face-to-face meeting with Kuei-shan, who perhaps has heard of Te-shan's reputation and is wary of this guest. Without such a meeting, Te-shan's visit to the temple is a failure. He has neither found a mentor nor has demonstrated his superiority. On his return, his style is ceremonial and polite.

As for the abbot, at first it seems that Kuei-shan does not react. He withholds words when Te-shan stands before him and seems oblivious to the rival's comings and goings. In other koans, masters leave the temple to test hermits in caves or huts who are gaining a reputation that threatens the authority of the institutional leader. This would be like an executive or manager emerging out of his suite one fine day to examine a white collar who, he has heard, may be surpassing his level of productivity. But the executive also realizes that he is the one being tested by the upstart. Another image is Wild West hero Billy the Kid coming from his hideout to challenge a younger gunslinger. It also calls to mind a samurai Warrior testing his sword-fighting skills as he tries to baptize his weapon.

Kuei-shan appears inactive, but he is not just sitting still while the rival attacks. Neither does he let himself be surprised into a state of panic when threatened by the newcomer. The commentary says,

- *He's watching that fellow with steely eyes. It takes someone like this to grab a tiger by the whiskers.*

Calmly observing events unfold, he lets Te-shan reveal his true colors before issuing a response. Kuei-shan's demeanor creates an invisible shield. He does not let himself be forced into a quick reaction he would later regret. According to a Zen saying,

- *The mind is a citadel that needs to be protected by the soldiers (senses).*

Kuei-shan is defending not only his temple and his authority, but also the integrity and dignity of the Mind that stands behind them.

In the first segment of the koan, Te-shan has an inner dialogue but the conversation with the master is a one-word, one-way monologue. Holding up the mat, he addresses the abbot as "Teacher," which is quite a contrast with his previous behavior. This may be intended to serve as an apology or to further provoke Kuei-shan

Pai-chang holding the fly-whisk while sitting on the high seat.

by seeming to patronize him. Kuei-shan remains impassive and reacts by reaching for his **fly-whisk**. This ritual implement, a holdover from pre-Buddhist shamanism in China where it was used in purification and exorcism rites, is the main symbol of authority wielded by a Zen master as he sits on a throne in the Dharma Hall.

The fly-whisk not only represents status but often serves as a teaching instrument when masters use it to draw circles in the air or toss it down on the ground. It is also instilled with magical powers, changing into a dragon or flying up to the heavens.

Here, the fly-whisk is Kuei-shan's instrument of nonverbal communication by which he asserts his control in the face of a mighty challenge from the newcomer. He is pulling rank. Both the arrogant and the submissive utterances of Te-shan have tested his patience, and he resorts to a symbol that conveys power. This device has its limits. Ultimately, according to Zen, all symbols are merely physical objects that cannot embody genuine authority. If used in a hollow or arbitrary way, they are just as useless as words, which cannot actually be the thing they refer to.

Te-shan is apparently flustered by the show of Kuei-shan's power. The act of shaking his sleeves is a way of expressing disdain and reasserting his own claim. At this point in the narrative, the reader is uncertain about Te-shan's status. Has he failed miserably or succeeded spectacularly? The commentary again calls him a wild fox, but also says he is uniquely skilled at "grasping the cloudy mist," or knowing ultimate reality.

With symbols clashing, Te-shan shows he is willing to disregard Kuei-shan's superior status. By resorting to the ritual device, the abbot has not demonstrated his superiority but confirmed Te-shan's self-image as unique and autonomous. No longer brash or arrogant, Te-shan summons the true meaning of anti-structure by mustering the courage to walk away from the scene. He realizes at that moment he is probably seen as a loner and loser by the members of Kuei-shan's community. Yet the way people perceive things can change if he is able to establish authority and has the patience to wait for results.

A verse commentary compares Te-shan to a warrior who, captured while making a daring raid behind enemy lines, is able to escape through a surprise maneuver:

- *Like the famed general entering behind enemy lines,*
  Then making a narrow escape,
  Te-shan sets off on a mad dash,
  But is not left alone.
  Sitting amid the weeds on the summit of the solitary
  mountain peak—
  Lord have mercy!

This also shows that Te-shan's victory is not complete. "Sitting amid the weeds," suggests that his accomplishments remain partial and that his vision is still obstructed.

Kuei-shan might have cause to be upset by Te-shan's slight, but he ends by remarking that Te-shan will surpass all the Buddhas and Patriarchs. This suggests that by using outrageous anti-structural behavior or Beat Zen in an effective way, he is given due respect by the leading representative of the institutional structure or Square Zen. Beat Zen trumps Square Zen, although there are times when, as with Kuei-shan holding the fly-whisk, you may have to draw an imaginary square with your fingers as a way of holding the line against the intrusion of anti-structure. In the end, however, you realize that, a square in the air is not really there.

Kuei-shan is using a pedagogical method found in many medieval traditions worldwide and based on the apprenticeship model. The teacher almost never offers a positive evaluation of any disciple in front of other students. The silent treatment is an indirect method of teaching that inspires improvement in a group context and mitigates the egotism that can result in conflict. This is not because the teacher is turning his back on one of the troupe who has just given a great performance. Rather, silence helps the members of the group develop an ability to sense intuitively what the reactions of others really are, beyond a reliance on words and no-words.

The hierarchical pattern of Te-shan as underling and Kuei-shan as overlord has parallels in today's professional environment. Imagine you are Kuei-shan supervising a junior colleague whose talents and skills have probably deserved more support and recognition than he has actually received. One day, in frustration and with a show of bravado, he comes marching into your office, crossing from east to west and from west to east. Do you respond by evoking a symbol of authority comparable to the fly-whisk, for example, by picking up a document?

The koan narrative indicates that there are three key principles. The first is the necessity and unavoidability of the Encounter to determine truth in interpersonal interaction. Like Te-shan, the junior colleague will not be in a position to feel confident until he has gone through an exchange. The second principle is that you must take a step-by-step approach in building toward an Encounter. Skipping a step, as Te-shan does at first, can be a deadly mistake that will doom later strategies. Before breaking free from structure, it must be clear that you have tried all the other recourses and remedies supplied by the system.

The third principle is that beneath the surface conflict, in which they are the worst of rivals, Te-shan and Kuei-shan are the closest of allies. According to the koan commentary, Te-shan, who has a false start but is legitimated in the end, and Kuei-shan, who seems challenged but holds his own, are both exemplary of pulling the bow too late in committing tactical errors as well as setting strategy in motion by demonstrating authenticity. As neither one is simply correct or incorrect, they are leading each other toward truth. Following a noted Chinese saying,

- *Teaching and learning grow together.*

Only the Contestants Know for Sure

Both Confrontation and Encounter involve some kind of show-down, but the former is direct and one-dimensional, whereas the Encounter mobilizes and integrates diverse aspects of constructive engagement. In the mode of Confrontation, someone who may be vacillating or inconclusive is questioned in straightforward language,

• *Did you or didn't you … [fill in the blank, e.g., give me an unfair assignment; or favor someone else for the promotion]?*

One possibility is that you will get quick and helpful clarification of a thorny topic on which there has been a misunderstanding or lack of information. This can serve to clear the air. But it is more likely that the person challenged will be put on the defensive and provide an unclear or elusive response.

At the point that the attempt to gain a resolution through direct questioning proves ineffective, the Confrontation becomes unsatisfactory. While there is always a chance that it will end in victory, it often leads to defeat or stalemate. Years ago a football

ENCOUNTER	versus	CONFRONTATION
	Competition as	
Bird's-eye view		Personal gain
Flexibility		Insistence
Openendedness		Intimidation
Mutuality	**over**	Demands
Negotiation		Victory vs. Defeat
	Results in	
Indirect methods to	**over**	Direct challenge based
reach goals by creating		on aggressive or passive
reconciliation		attitudes
Cooperation and		Conflict and Discord
Ongoing Teamwork		Divisiveness

coach explained that he was reluctant to utilize the newly invented forward pass because,

- *Three things can happen [completion, incompletion, or interception], and two of them are bad.*

Of course, the forward pass eventually prevailed, but only by drastically changing the formation and game plan of the whole team. The running game is still used but no longer exclusively.

One time Senpai was approached by several junior colleagues who were doing high-quality work but felt that the institutional structure had them trapped in a marginal, vulnerable position. Their unit was not recognized as part of any of the main divisions, so they were left hanging, unprotected by an umbrella organization. They did not have, but were trying to recruit a strong leader who could look out for their interests and provide a clear channel to express their concerns or solicit support. This new leader could benefit from the work they produced.

The members of this unit told Senpai that they felt like Ronin without a senior colleague to take them under his wing. But they were a little naïve. They did not realize that to achieve this, they needed not only the support of one particular colleague, but also the approval of a high-level administrator. The administrator would have to take responsibility for rearranging the organizational structure in order to provide new resources either directly to this group or to a division with oversight over them. He would have to be convinced that it was worthwhile to expand his scope of operations and go to bat for this change.

Senpai gave them a heads up about the need to involve an administrator. Out of a combination of frustration and overeagerness, they took the liberty of calling upon a powerful vice president, who agreed to meet with them. At first, the VP seemed intrigued and interested. But it turned out that the juniors were unprepared for this meeting. When the VP asked tough questions about what they brought to the table and why he should invest his time and funds, they realized they did not have enough evidence to support their cause. They gave the impression of being a bit desperate and unreasonably demanding. They were unable either to step back to a higher level of intuitive awareness and provide an overview or to offer concessions out of a position of strength that would have built a sense of trust and cooperation.

The difference between Confrontation and Encounter can be seen by comparing the terms "pressure" and "leverage." The former implies trying to use some form of threat, coercion, or intimidation from the outside that will compel a recalcitrant colleague or tempestuous rival to do your bidding. Leverage, however, suggests that with agility and aplomb you apply the gentle but persistent and effective action of a lever from within the system to bring about a new, more elevated level of understanding beyond intrigue and contestation.

Like Te-shan at the beginning of the koan, these Ronin had approached the corridors of power too quickly while lacking the leverage with which to maneuver in the negotiation. The discussion was clearly leading to a Confrontation, in which they could only ask defensively, "Why aren't you willing to help us out?" They were unable to recover and turn the meeting into an Encounter in which there would be constructive give-and-take, so they quietly withdrew their request and eventually each member had to go a separate way.

An alternative to the modalities of Confrontation and Encounter is the Great Compromise, which in many instances is a useful approach to achieving harmony. However, when compromise ends in vacillation or ambiguity it is less than effective. Unlike Confrontation, which pushes too hard too fast, compromise may not try at all. The junior colleagues could have chosen to wait passively for options to unfold but in the end this would not have had better results than forcing the issue. Zen calls for a middle way between aggressive and passive attitudes, which is often achieved through anti-structural behavior.

Consider the case of King Solomon, who refused to compromise with the two women who both claimed to be a baby's mother. By utilizing anti-structural elements to create an Encounter in demanding that the infant be cut in half, Solomon devised a way through which the real mother was identified because she would rather give the baby up than see it harmed. In an anecdote about monks who were arguing about the ownership of a cat, Zen master Nan-chuan one-ups Solomon, actually cutting the cat in half!

In a sequel to this koan, Chao-chou, upon hearing of what happened to the cat, puts his shoes on his head backwards and walks away in anti-structural fashion that outdoes Nan-chuan. The master calls out that if only Chao-chou, who shows himself indifferent to argumentation, had been there during the dispute, the cat would have been saved. In the strategies of Solomon and Nan-chuan, compromise based on direct inquiry is considered insufficient to uncover the truth and bring an end to an impasse. Instead, these two figures test the Mind from the standpoint of intuition at the brink of anti-structure. Exposing the attitudes and intentions of the contestants beneath their artifice or pretense is a creative way to resolve a crisis.

Switching Heads and Changing Faces

Prevailing in an Encounter means being ready for an all-stops-pulled-out, eyeball-to-eyeball meeting, in which self-discipline and self-control are tested in the face of strenuous challenges to an ability to assert authority. Nothing stands between you and your competitor or partner. All other factors and considerations dissolve into the background of what is spoken and unspoken.

The Encounter is not a specific meeting, a single event, or set of exchanges. Ordinary time stops, the clock is thrown out the window, and there is an opportunity, however long or short it may last, to create a resolution. The sense of how long something takes to happen is relative to the inner experience of timing encompassing both recollections and anticipation.

According to a comment on the Te-shan koan,

- *Switching heads and changing faces, he stirs up waves even though there is no wind.*

Bold moves and maneuvers are required when crossing over invisible lines into an open arena where integrity and commitment, rather than hierarchy and status, determine worth and power. Genuine authority is not revealed by this or that word, thought, symbol, or deed, but in everything about the way a person speaks, thinks, and acts.

When meeting with the supervisor in the case of the unwanted assignment, for example, having prepared a set speech or composed a memo in your mind may well inhibit the ability to react and respond effectively and persuasively to what he is saying on the spot. It is preferable to exude a sense of authority about your abilities and clarity about what it is you want and need that is compatible with his requirements and expectations.

If you are well prepared and confident that you have created the necessary advantage, no one, single strategy is paramount. Because the Unmoving Mind is able to react in various ways, traditional Zen masters are thoroughly unpredictable yet unflappable, keeping contestants and rivals wondering what is going to come next. This calls for a flexibility that constantly adjusts methods and movements in response to different people and circumstances that can be characterized as the "strategy of no strategy." According to a Zen koan,

- *If you have a staff, I will give you a staff. If you have no staff, I will take away your staff.*

Strategic ambiguity and surprise, feinting and reversal are some of the indirect techniques utilized by the Mind, according to accounts in koans and Art of War writings. These methods, which borrow Fox techniques for Buddha intentions, call to mind the world of high-stakes poker, which requires skills that take advantage of the uncertainty and vulnerability of opponents. The card player takes great risks while using a variety of decoys, bluffs, and diverse ways of ambushing or trapping the other players—all the while concealing the strength of his own hand by keeping a "poker face." Indirect techniques are particularly effective when rooted in an attitude of neutrality, which holds back emotion and lets the intentions of peers and rivals be revealed.

The Unmoving Mind maximizes strengths and minimizes weaknesses by exerting the least effort and conserving sources of power. During the Encounter, it may be necessary to shift positions or retreat from preconceived notions. That is why Te-shan is described as "a famed general entering through enemy lines." When a Warrior sees an opponent's weakness or vulnerability, that is not where he attacks. Everyone else will seize the chance to go after a weakness. There is nothing to be gained by competing with so many others. Instead, the Warrior attacks the strength, which has been left untended by the opponent who concentrates his defense where he is weak. This tactic is expressed by the koan's comment,

- *Nothing can stop him from cutting off the tongues of everyone in the world.*

According to Art of War, being ambiguous means that if someone is a little too eager for a breakthrough to happen, make them wait a little longer than desired. Or, if someone puts up too much resistance, try to push it on them more quickly. There are also times for undertaking the exact opposite strategies by forcing things on the impatient or withholding from the reluctant. Any strategy will backfire if it becomes stale and predictable, so you must be prepared to reverse the pattern. Zen masters, knowing that they are bound to encounter surprises and inconsistencies, welcome or unwelcome, need to be ready to handle all contingencies as they unfold. Therefore,

- *The strategy of no strategy is still a strategy.*

Reacting in the Moment is like being at your best in athletics. Sports contests demand the spontaneity, discipline, and mutually transformational quality of the Encounter. One's performance can only be determined and evaluated through interaction with an opponent. Practicing a tennis serve, a baseball pitch, or a soccer kick for endless hours with an inanimate backstop can be a useful training. Ultimately, however, the quality of the serve, pitch, or kick is to be judged by the response, or lack of it, in the opposing player at the height of the contest.

Although the event may take place in a public forum under the eyes of spectators and with the support of teammates, the result comes down to one-on-one, whoever flinches or blinks first loses. They say the pitcher's mound in Yankee Stadium is the loneliest place in the world. Yet, the opponents can help bring each other to higher levels of performance. In the end, who is the winner and who is the loser? Holding up his gold medal, Olympic decathlon champion Bruce Jenner said,

- *I love my competitor; he brings out the best in me.*

This reminds us of rivalry between boxers Mohammed Ali and Joe Frazier, who were often said to bring out the best in each other in the ring (though unfortunately the worst outside of it).

Just as in slamming a home run or stroking a winner in tennis, for a successful Encounter what is needed is an action completed in an artless, spontaneous, effortless way without taking time for the use of reason. Despite thoughtful and calculated preparation, the Moment of implementation itself must have the immediacy of an instinct or a reflex freed from the problems of an automatic, conditioned response. Its efficacy depends on an intuitive awareness that is integrated with conscious, deliberate thinking. The swing of the bat cannot be a divided effort in which calculation and action struggle against one another. As Tom Kasulis explains it, the aim of Zen is to make reaction time instantaneous. It is technically accurate to say, "I hit the baseball," but,

- *At the moment of the original event, there is only an unbroken hitting-of-the-baseball.*

For this Moment, there is no ego or "I" to stop you from acting spontaneously:

- *The batter best performs by not thinking about hitting—that is, not by reflecting on what was learned or on what must be done, but rather by simply being alert.*

An unconditional and fearless sense of self-worth leads to success in hitting the ball under the pressure of high stakes.

According to the sword master Takuan Soho, knowing what to do and what not to do is the key to self-control:

- *The accomplished man uses the sword...When it is necessary to kill, he kills. When it is necessary to give life, he gives life. When killing, he kills in complete concentration; when giving life, he gives life in complete concentration. Without looking at right and wrong, he is able to see right and wrong; without attempting to discriminate, he is able to discriminate well.*

When the ball needs to be hit the batter strikes it and when the batter wants to wait out the pitch he refrains from striking it.

Imagine an executive responding on a case-by-case basis to each and every employee. He explores personnel issues from a variety of angles without coming to a fixed conclusion that would cut off the possibility for constructive change. If circumstances require using the sword (or Mind) to kill (or criticize scathingly), he uses the sword that way. If they require him to give life (or praise effusively) he uses the sword for that purpose. He can change paths or reverse his direction in midstream, if that is what is called for, because the Unmoving Mind provides an underlying constancy.

Acting offers another useful analogy to the Encounter, not so much acting in films where you get the chance to have "do-overs," but in live theatrical performance in which everything is immediate and nothing is left on the cutting room floor. The Zen view is epitomized by the director who at the dress rehearsal before the opening night of a play on which all their hopes were riding, exhorted his anxious troupe,

- *Stop acting, and ... Act!*

If the actor misses a cue or is unprepared or ineffectual in any way there is no filter to prevent this from coming through to the audience and critics. That is why some Hollywood actors hone their craft by returning to the rigors of Broadway between films. When something goes awry, improvisation can in some special cases be just as effective as the script. If your Mind is steady, then taking a risk by delivering a line in a novel way can turn out well in the end.

A Tale of Two "Greats"

The initial moment when the supervisor offers the unwanted assignment demonstrates Encounter interaction. In that tiny instant, the most effective reaction can be as simple yet as convincing as, "Great, I'll do it." Furthermore, you can add,

- *In fact, I have some ideas on how to make the project more ambitious, and if given the necessary resources I can motivate and integrate the whole unit. Step One is to interview and analyze, and write an assessment report. The next step is implementation.*

By accepting the new unit as a positive opportunity for expansion rather than as an impediment to personal success, you work with the supervisor to develop a base of mutual support.

You may find in the coming days that your budget and staff are increased, and your prestige elevated. How did you get this far so soon? How can this success be understood and replicated in other instances?

The first question is, Why is this "Great, I'll do it" so distinct and superior to the "Great, I'll do it" that was discussed in chapter 2 as an example of a deficient response based on passivity and lack of choice? If you just look at the words themselves, the responses seem identical. However, persuasive communication is not only about words but the intention that lies behind the way you speak. The first "Great, I'll do it" really means the opposite. You feel trapped and cannot think of anything to do but acquiesce.

The second "Great, I'll do it" reflects the power of speaking to gain what is fair and reasonable, and transmutes a conflictive situation into constructive dialogue and negotiation. Words flowing not from intimidation or pressure but from free will and composure at the borderline of anti-structure alter everyone's perception of the structure of the workplace environment. The key point about the second "Great" is that you could have chosen not to say this or to say it in a completely different way. While this phrasing is not radically anti-structural on the scale of kicking over a water pitcher or cutting off a limb, asserting your confidence and clout help overcome the impasse and attain anticipated results.

The move from a preoccupation with the past to a focus on the present helps put an end to delays and realize goals that were starting to seem out of reach. What needs to be done? First, create a report that assesses the status of the unit assigned to you; then hold a series of individual and group meetings to culminate in a set of recommendations about restructuring. The support you will need from your peers can be garnered only through meetings in which all sides are given a chance to air their views and suggest solutions. Everyone must come to terms with the recommendations before they are implemented. By treating each member of the unit with the same respect you would like to receive from your supervisor, you serve as an example. You show your colleagues how to contribute to overall unity and productivity for the sake of completing a project as an end in itself, rather than just for the benefit of a particular group of individuals. It is a case of sharing the ownership while taking full responsibility.

The way of Encounter is similarly useful in striking a balance between being aggressive and succumbing to external pressures so that you are able to transform the delayed promotion into a grand opportunity. Instead of going over the head of the vice president, the party responsible for the decision, on a side issue concerning procedures, you request a meeting to discuss the substance and vision of current projects. Although you care deeply and are prepared for the topic of the promotion to be raised, you do not ask the VP where things stand with the search, which would reflect a preoccupation with gaining status over demonstrating stature and integrity. The less said the better. Instead, showing that you are committed to continuing your efforts conscientiously and wholeheartedly, undistracted by petty concerns about income or outcome, makes it clear that you deserve the elevation in status.

Meanwhile, you have a chance to get a better idea of what the vice president is looking for in a candidate and the responsibilities the new position entails. As expected, this fails to land you the new job right away, but you have demonstrated that you are a team player, reasonable and self-assured.

By demonstrating restraint and self-discipline, you encourage others to rally and communicate the right message on your behalf. A positive, productive attitude mobilizes sympathy and support among colleagues at all levels, and the vice president is primed to give you a receptive hearing the next time you propose an exciting project. She is impressed when she sees that instead of letting yourself get stuck in a dead end with no outlet you take a "don't get even, get to work" approach. Influenced by support for your cause from both administrators and rank-and-file, the vice president is persuaded to reopen the search and you eventually succeed in gaining the promotion.

CHAPTER SEVEN

All's Well that Ends Well

S ENPAI OUTLINED FOUR STEPS that build to a successful Encounter. The steps are a template for spontaneous yet deliberate
behavior that integrates and coordinates inner reality, or the
levels of consciousness, by using words and silence effectively to
refashion intractable institutional structure. Within each of the
four steps, there is a time to let go of convention as well as a time

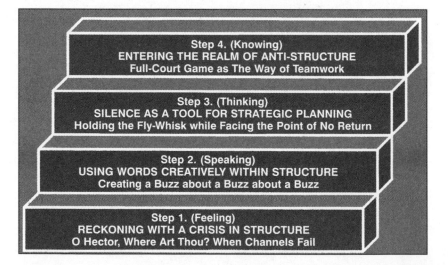

Step 4. (Knowing)
ENTERING THE REALM OF ANTI-STRUCTURE
Full-Court Game as The Way of Teamwork

Step 3. (Thinking)
SILENCE AS A TOOL FOR STRATEGIC PLANNING
Holding the Fly-Whisk while Facing the Point of No Return

Step 2. (Speaking)
USING WORDS CREATIVELY WITHIN STRUCTURE
Creating a Buzz about a Buzz about a Buzz

Step 1. (Feeling)
RECKONING WITH A CRISIS IN STRUCTURE
O Hector, Where Art Thou? When Channels Fail

to stay within structure. According to the opening comments in the Te-shan koan, the bottom line is to be able to "administer medicine appropriate to the conditions," yet the question remains,

• *Now tell me, is it better to release or to hold firm?*

Trapped in a crisis at the beginning of Step One but before leaping to Step Four and the realm of anti-structure, you try to bring about change within the standpoint of accepting the conditions of conventional structure by juggling and choosing the appropriate use of speech and silence:

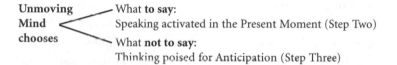

Unmoving Mind chooses — What to say: Speaking activated in the Present Moment (Step Two) — What not to say: Thinking poised for Anticipation (Step Three)

Speaking conceals even as it reveals and silence reveals while concealing. There are opportunities for speaking and for refraining from speech. The mastery of both is essential for persuasive communication and constructive negotiation.

When the avenues of speaking and not speaking have been tried but fail to obtain results in the first three steps, it may be useful to break free and cultivate "strange deeds" of anti-structure in the final step. At the most intense moment of the Encounter, both parties will have crossed over an invisible line of hierarchy that previously separated them. They stand in an open realm of immediacy, in which there are no distinctions or distractions. Each of the participants in the dialogue has the chance to convey his or her depth of understanding with a bold and compelling statement. Lines of authority and reliance on security and safety nets are set aside for the sake of a leap into an unknown world where change and ingenuity prevail, as when Kuei-shan kicked over the water pitcher or Te-shan stomped out of the Dharma Hall. How do you get there?

Step One

RECKONING WITH A CRISIS IN STRUCTURE
(Feeling)

You begin by recognizing and investigating the causes of a break-down in structure and seeking an effective remedy. When a problem arises that obstructs your agenda, first determine whether what seems like a setback is a legitimate crisis to be overcome or represents the temporary dominance of a valuable alternative view that must be appreciated despite contradicting your perspective.

According to a traditional Buddhist parable from the *Lotus Sutra* known as "The Parable of the Burning House," a father returns home to find the house ablaze, with his children trapped on the second floor playing with their toys and oblivious to the flames. As he sees the crisis that the children do not recognize, he must design a strategy to free them from danger just in time. In that vein, the first step can be referred to as "Seeing the Fire." To maintain credibility, however, you must avoid the "sky is falling" syndrome of distortion, exaggeration, and hyperbole. It is crucial to be able to know that when there is smoke there is fire, but it is also prohibited to cry "fire" in a crowded theater.

Once you identify an obstacle to achievement and begin trying to deal with it, you realize that the organizational status quo tends to produce delays or arbitrary and counterproductive alterations that stand in the way of finding a solution. Everything negotiated or transacted is a trade-off at best. As the Te-shan koan suggests,

- *He kept the hat covering his head, but lost the shoes covering his feet.*

If you give in to your emotions and express frustration and futility or passivity and compliance, you are drawing the bow after the thief has fled by trading off one set of problems wrought by extraneous circumstances for another set internally generated. Instead, hold a steady course and go through proper channels, allowing everyone in the chain of command an opportunity to develop a way to resolve the crisis, even if this tests your patience.

While awaiting results that are being processed through investigating external mechanisms and measures, such as budget accounts, distribution data, sales reports, and other indicators of productivity, the Unmoving Mind avoids getting distracted. It maintains a balance of composure and spontaneity, neither giving in to impatience nor letting the agony of uncertainty drag on indefinitely. Stay focused on the details of a constructive project while anticipating how to follow through, depending on the success or failure of current activities.

In some cases, channels themselves can offer protection and support. One of Senpai's assistants who had been quietly doing a very effective job all along suddenly made a spectacular effort that was deserving of a promotion and other rewards. Senpai double-checked procedures and budget. He had everything in order and submitted a request in time for a Thursday deadline. By the end of the day on Friday, he received notification from the division director of a freeze in personnel actions.

First thing on Monday morning, Senpai got a phone call from Human Resources that made him look pretty silly for having put in a request for a promotion that went against the directive. When Senpai put down the phone he thought to himself, "What did I do wrong and how can I compensate?" and then scratched his head for a while trying to sort out the various strands of the revolting development.

Then he realized that the sequence of events made the case for him. He called HR back and explained that when his request was put through there was no indication that a freeze was about to be announced. The request should therefore be honored. HR was not in a position to approve the hire but they could reopen the process. Sign-off would be required from upstairs. This would mean eventually having to negotiate with the parties responsible for the directive. Citing the unfairness of what had happened at the initial stage of going through routine channels would become a weapon Senpai could use as he moved to the next steps in the sequence to the Encounter.

O HECTOR, WHERE ART THOU?
WHEN CHANNELS FAIL

Organizational structure can be liberating and expansive but it also can become claustrophobic and constraining when people are crudely indifferent rather than acting with lofty neutrality. As George Harrison says of the "Taxman," the System can be harsh and unforgiving:

- *If you drive your car, I'll tax the street,*
  If you try to walk, I'll tax the street.

Channels are notoriously clogged arteries. Often, there is just one person who is in charge or who knows about a particular procedure or activity. If you can find out who the right someone is, you have to hope that they are not away from their desk or out to lunch or otherwise unresponsive.

A colleague told me the following story: She had placed an important order but it got backed up for weeks, while her deadline for spending the funds was rapidly running out. She would soon be in default and would have to return unspent monies to the funding agency because the most ordinary procedure had not been completed by the bureaucracy in her firm. Every time she complained, parties in different departments all said that she should not worry because they had "e-mailed Hector." Whoever Hector was, he must have had an important role and would surely be the one to resolve the problem, she was told. Time went by and there was still no definitive response. A crisis was looming. She decided to make a couple of well-placed phone calls to push matters along.

Finally, a senior associate who was in a position to know the scene (and whom she had only reluctantly approached) phoned back to assure her he had gotten to the bottom of the problem. He said he was able to offer advice that would straighten the situation out. She waited breathlessly and then sighed when he proudly announced the solution:

- *E-mail Hector ...*

What would her next step be? Apparently locked in, she was not able to move forward but could also not stay put and did not want to fall back. Rather than going directly to the division head, she still needed to exhaust intermediate efforts, beginning with exploring alternatives and explaining to supporters the need to reform the system.

Step Two

USING WORDS CREATIVELY WITHIN STRUCTURE
(Speaking)

When channels fail, creative speaking can generate positive change by using the tremendous power of words to loosen the rigidity of current structure. Through the process of EPA, which overcomes reactions based on bias or self-doubt, the voice becomes a useful tool for articulating a vision that builds alliances while also offering criticisms in a compelling, cogent, and constructive way.

At the moment of experiencing doubt, you feel a gap as wide as the Grand Canyon between what your role is supposed to be and the way things are being treated. It is this shock that causes you to hesitate and second-guess. But structure is not something fixed and static. Understanding that structure is not immutable enables you to put aside that lost, dazed, and confused feeling. Words uttered, as well as those held back, are not just arbitrary symbols. Rather, they are a tool of effective communication that can close the gap between hope and reality by conveying to partners in negotiation what it is you are trying to achieve.

Because of the infiltration of unpurified feelings, speaking often has a negative, "poison pen" impact. Confucius cautions about the destructive power of words,

- *A gentleman kills with the pen, an average man with spoken words, and a lesser man with stones.*

Similarly, according to a Dylan lyric,

- *Now, a very great man once said*
  That some people rob you with a fountain pen.
  It didn't take too long to find out
  Just what he was talkin' about.
  A lot of people don't have much food on their table,
  But they got a lot of forks n' knives,
  And they gotta cut somethin'.

Constructive criticism can be valuable, but if words are delivered in a way that causes embarrassment or humiliation, they can have a boomerang effect. There are a limitless array of phrases to select from, ranging from "this work is no good" to "let's see a little improvement." In some cases it is not the content but the style of speaking that counts. The words themselves are suitable but their impact is undermined or diminished if they are delivered in a mocking or condescending tone. The ideas may be appropriate but have a minimal effect if the person leaves muttering,

- *I didn't mind what was said, but why couldn't they have found a different way to say it?*

The words formed in your mind often come out of your mouth differently than you intended, whether you realize it or not. Do you find that you alter your tone and inflection based on whether, underneath it all, you like or dislike, care about or disregard the person?

A colleague who has made known his complaints, which, though legitimate, are too forcefully expressed may be dismissed by his supervisor as a "whiner." Yet, it is the administrator who has given up the position of moral authority in failing to take the opportunity to say,

- *I appreciate your interests and would like to address them, but they must be considered in light of the group.*

Sometimes what is said sounds convincing but is, at bottom, disingenuous and insincere. The Fox can mimic a speech pattern that pleases and soothes the soul, despite its falseness. The myth of the ravishing song of the Sirens illustrates the power to deceive and deter that is embedded in all forms of communication.

The opposite of this occurs when the words seem too revealing despite attempts to cover one's feelings. One time on *I Love Lucy*, Mrs. Lucy Ricardo, after telling countless fibs, took a vow that from then on she would speak only the truth. Then Lucy and Ethel visited a friend whose apartment was decorated with bric-a-brac from China. When the hostess went into another room Lucy remarked to Ethel that the place "looked like a nightmare after eating bad Chinese food." The friend returned and Ethel asked Lucy to tell her how she felt about the apartment. She responded, true to her vow, that it was "like a dream." This foil worked momentarily until Ethel said,

- *Tell her what kind of dream it was, Lucy.*

Speaking with honesty to a fault may win the moment and lose the day. Ronald Reagan was known as the tax-cutting president but actually oversaw some of the biggest tax increases in history. He just knew not to talk too much about it. At the 1984 Democratic convention, his challenger, Walter Mondale, who lost in a land-slide, said in his acceptance speech that because of budget deficits he would raise taxes. In fact, he remarked, "Both of us will raise taxes. The difference is that my opponent won't tell you. I just did." He was right. The rest, as they say, is history.

Words can be used to soothe the soul or torment it. My men-tor, who was Chinese, would always preface his criticism with praise. The principle seemed to be,

- *The greater the praise, the greater the criticism.*

So, when he called me in for a meeting, if the laudatory prefatory compliments lasted more than a few minutes, I knew I was in deep trouble.

CREATING A BUZZ
ABOUT A BUZZ ABOUT A BUZZ

On the positive side, the word, whether spoken or written, is said to have the remarkable ability to awaken divine energy. This is rec-ognized by religious traditions around the world, which empha-size various forms of prayer, chanting, and singing as methods of petitioning powers for benefits or forgiveness. In Mahayana Bud-dhism, for example, the merits of the *Lotus Sutra* are evoked by reading or copying, or even just reciting the title or chanting key passages of the scripture. This has a mysterious efficacy akin to Zen meditation for developing concentration and contemplation.

According to legend, the prayers of Kuya Shonin, a Japanese Buddhist saint, communicated spiritual truth so effectively that in a famous icon he is depicted with Buddhas appearing on the tip of his tongue.

Confucianism suggests that words have "magical" powers if we use this term in a very practical, down-to-earth rather than super-natural sense. Picture yourself seated at a long dinner table. You

Buddhist saint Kuya Shonin chanting prayers.

need to salt your food, but the saltshaker is at the opposite end of the table. Ask for it politely by just saying the one word, "please," and the salt seems to appear instantly without your having to get up or lift a finger. This is an example of changing structure through the creative use of speaking. Skip the politeness, and you may never get the shaker unless you go over yourself and pick it up.

If something unpleasant would happen at the meal, like a sneeze, belch, or hiccup, an "excuse me" would clear the air, metaphorically speaking. However, although simple everyday expressions like "please" and "thanks" can have a significant impact, they can also cause a backlash if used insincerely, as when a customer service representative who has been completely unhelpful closes by telling you mechanically to "Have a nice day."

The use of words to rearrange structure can be referred to as **Daijobu Diplomacy**—*daijobu* is a Japanese term meaning "all is well." This is the useful technique of expressing a positive, upbeat message, which alleviates constraints and elevates all parties without being Pollyannaish or unrealistic. Daijobu is a matter of "Fighting Fire with Fire." In the "Parable of the Burning House," in order to lure the children away from danger as quickly as possible, the father calls out that he can offer them fine chariots, in other words, better playthings than they already have. This is a successful method for averting the disaster of losing the children to the conflagration.

A traditional Chinese Art of War saying captures the goal of Daijobu Diplomacy,

- *Make flowers bloom in the tree.*

Even if the tree is dying and the branches are bare, people are made to feel that blossoms are flourishing. This technique works like jujitsu. The obstacle of ingrained institutional indifference or negativity is turned to your advantage when hidden Buddhas are motivated to support your efforts. It is important to note that a Buddha is one who is genuinely appreciative and convinced of the merits of your work, whereas an ally needs to feel there is something to gain, as well as nothing to lose, in advancing your cause. A Buddha is indifferent in the positive sense of evaluating quality alone without regard to the distractions of status and hierarchy.

In using speech to bring about concrete changes in the world, the underlying principle is,

- *Perception is reality.*

Some people can talk your ears off and others shoot from the lip, but Zen develops finesse with words great and small. As expressed by a traditional Zen verse, the aim of Daijobu Diplomacy is to alter perception purposefully by putting an appropriate spin on the situation:

- *Hundreds of flowers in spring, the moon in autumn,*
  A cool breeze in summer, and snow in winter.
  If your mind is not clouded by vanity,
  Then for you every single day is a good time of the year.

Daijobu Diplomacy means that when confused about another's motives—for example, if their response to your queries or initiatives is vague or unclear—you continue to act in a calm and steady manner that shows confidence in your agenda. Daijobu proceeds "as if," in the sense of the Kantian categorical imperative, there is already a sense of certainty and inevitability to your plans. This draws your erstwhile challenger away from obstructive intentions and towards a focus on accomplishing results for the common good.

Senpai had an interesting experience with a colleague who was quietly supporting his efforts on a potential breakthrough project. The colleague was someone who knew the ins and outs of the approval process, having been both a candidate and a judge of the competition, and went out of his way to make himself available to give advice. As the waiting dragged on for weeks, the colleague politely asked Senpai every couple of days if he had heard any news, lending hope and support without making him feel anxious. Then, when the good news finally came, the colleague was mysteriously missing in action. Was it the "J word"—jealousy—that intervened?

Just a short time later, the same colleague received encouraging news about something he was working on. Senpai made a point of being first in line to congratulate him. Although he was tempted by tit for tat, Senpai did not want to be guilty of the same flaw as the colleague. In the long run the payoff would be continued collaboration with a valuable associate. Senpai's thesis is that All's Well that Ends Well. The rough spots along the way are simply dues that have to be paid.

The effectiveness of Daijobu Diplomacy depends on three main features. First, it opens up dialogue by avoiding insistence, threats, or demands and offers a boundless set of options. If you want a supervisor to reverse a negative evaluation of your work, do not complain or blame others or force the issue at an inopportune time. Speaking up in a way that won't be seen as petty or vindictive wins the day. This does far more to impress those whose opinion counts than the kind of behavior that feeds conflict and prevents the proverbial ox's tail from getting through the window. Colleagues will not feel threatened or see a challenge to their own agendas but will welcome the chance to participate in resolving a crisis. With Daijobu, all those who deserve it can claim at least some of the credit for reaching a mutual understanding.

The second feature is that Daijobu Diplomacy stimulates thoughts that may not otherwise come to fruition, and yields ideas that are as beautiful yet fragile as flowers swaying in the spring breeze. A key maneuver is **Creating a Buzz about a Buzz**. If you realize that people are generally not enthusiastic about your planning and there is no buzz suggesting that the project is taking hold, you may seek to create an atmosphere that makes others feel there is great interest. They may then get excited about the excitement. Eventually this can lead people to embrace your concept and promote the strengths of a previously overlooked project. You've heard, "If you build it, they will come." In this case,

- *Talk about building and someone will help you build it. Then they will come.*

Senpai had a Japanese friend, who early in his career was struggling to succeed in the very difficult Japanese university system. A doctorate is awarded relatively late in your career in Japan, especially in institutions that still follow the older system, and you generally have to wait for someone to retire before you can get a permanent job. As in America, the main requirement for good standing is the publication of a major research volume, but the production costs of the elegant, boxed Japanese publications are so high that books sell for a couple of hundred dollars per copy. The young professor decided to create a buzz about himself that would launch his career by sending a complimentary copy of his book to hundreds of his colleagues in Japan and abroad. This meant an investment (and bank loan) of close to $100K, which ultimately was worth going into debt for the long-term payoff of getting the good word out and enhancing his status.

In another example, Senpai led an initiative that everyone liked. But nobody supported it in a meaningful way by providing resources needed to carry it out. It would have been an easy choice to roll over and play dead. Instead, he looked for every scrap of interest or enthusiasm that anybody expressed and communicated to everyone else what each of these people had said. Time went by without much promise for success. One day a visitor came to the office saying her supervisor had heard about the project and wanted to be on board before the train left the station. This was sufficient support to get the initiative going and eventually the necessary resources were found. By not giving in to the reality of dead trees and the apparently unchangeable quality of structure, Senpai was able to make flowers bloom and achieve a great innovation.

The third feature of Daijobu Diplomacy involves holding your creative side in check. It is important to stay realistic and pragmatic and refrain from spinning fantasies. Stick to the facts, do not violate the basic truths. Be sure that you are not alone in your interpretation and that you are taking into account all other possible perspectives, without letting misguided assumptions crop up like weeds as supposed "facts," which in the end will lead to a loss of credibility.

In one case, Senpai had a colleague who violated the rules of Daijobu by overstepping the bounds of appropriate discourse. This gentleman knew a lot about a lot of things, but like most of us, he really only knew a whole lot about just a couple of things. In his mind, there was a basic confusion about what he knew a lot about and what he really knew a whole lot about. The confusion was exposed whenever he talked too much about what he only knew a lot about in front of someone who knew a whole lot more about the same thing.

He should have heeded the cautionary note of philosopher Martin Heidegger, who said in a book called *What is This Thing We Call Thinking?*

• *A thinker thinks only one thought.*

The negative buzz started up that this individual did not know what he was talking about because he had too many thoughts. The poet Verlaine once said that some ideas are like vermin. They must be stomped on so that only the worthy thoughts survive and develop into articulated expression. Be careful about what you project. Loss of credibility on one issue can have a devastating effect on the way you are received across the board.

Step Three

SILENCE AS A TOOL FOR STRATEGIC PLANNING
(Thinking)

The aim of Daijobu Diplomacy is to use speaking to help prevent misperceptions and gain attention for your creative efforts. But in the final analysis words are always a bit deceptive, as are all symbols. According to a Zen saying,

- *A painted rice cake does not satisfy hunger.*

You can paint a beautiful picture or eloquently describe a scrumptious cookie to set the stage and inspire, but what happens when you want to take a bite? A picture may be worth a thousand words. But, are a thousand pictures worthwhile if they do not correspond to reality?

Even the most exquisite words grow flat and stale if not backed up by the authority that only bottom-line results can bring. Felicitous speaking may create a good feeling about a proposal but it does not necessarily bring about the desired alteration of structure. Nothing is sadder than eloquence reduced to mere repetition, inconsistency, or incongruity.

I once had a supervisor whom many people described as a "Southern gentleman." He was always very well dressed and well spoken. He liked to say that he could,

- *Charm the spots off of a cow.*

But I never did see them spots go anywhere. Talk is cheap, as we can see from the failure of Te-shan's proclaiming, in effect, "I win," at the beginning of the koan narrative. He then realized that actions speak louder than words and are more effective than pictures. You can talk the talk, but at some point, it is meaningless unless you also walk the walk.

A commentator who interviewed leading representatives of the Zen tradition in Japan kept hearing them discuss whether someone had attained a state of enlightenment or entered into Nirvana. He started to ponder the difference between this state and an ordinary, unenlightened condition. How can you really say which is which?

Riding on the bullet train from Tokyo to Kyoto and hurdling past the distant, snow-capped peak of Mt. Fuji, as well as over-built urban and suburban neighborhoods, he reflected on what it means to say,

- *I am in Nirvana.*

Is Nirvana a state of bliss that can be experienced at any moment there is a Satori? Or, perhaps Satori is an instantaneous break-through, while Nirvana is a more enduring level of realization? Wondering whether perhaps he was in Nirvana he realized,

- *I'm not in Nirvana. I'm "in" a train.*

It doesn't do any good to keep talking about Nirvana. You have either got it or not. Debating what it means probably only high-lights that you ain't there yet.

Another limitation of the Daijobu approach is that there are bound to be times when you convince yourself that you are in the right because you go over the conversation in your own mind or with people who are familiar with your viewpoint and have an ulterior motive for sounding sympathetic. But when an idea is discussed with the relevant parties, the compelling quality of the argument goes up in smoke. A similar problem is when just a bit too much is said that exposes a weakness or opens up a flank to attack, creating the perception of vulnerability. This is the time to stand back and reassess.

Similarly, Creating a Buzz is not enough in itself to achieve effective change. Words after all are empty containers. They must be accompanied and complemented by other methods and tech-niques for bringing the Encounter to fruition. The attitude of All's Well that Ends Well recognizes the limits of speech and leads back to the patient readiness of no-words that waits and watches. When the effectiveness of verbal communication has run its course, embrace the path of remaining silent, which is a form of thinking that does not rely on the crutch of words. Sometimes it is better to "Fight Fire Without Fire."

NAVIGATING THE CROSSROADS

Standing at the brink of conflict, you occupy a crossroads. You realize that you have accomplished everything possible by speaking and that continuing to push in the same direction will only backfire. When one more e-mail to Hector proves useless and you know in your heart of hearts that another attempt to Create a Buzz will not produce fruit but only blossoms that will quickly fade and scatter, awareness of reaching a dead end drives you to move on to discover other pathways.

The principle of progression, of exhausting the possibilities in one stage before attempting to move on to the next stage, is particularly important in the transition from the role of speaking in Step Two to the use of silence in Step Three. The Zen critique of the father in the parable of the burning house who, in order to avert catastrophe, calls out a promise to the children that he may not be able to deliver is that false hope and illusion easily becomes a crutch. While speaking may offer a wonderful reprieve that is necessary in some cases, the opposite use of silence is a tool that forces the other party to develop a greater degree of self-reliance and self-control.

Using words and using no-words may seem like opposites, however they are very closely connected. Silence does not reverse but rather extends the approach of speaking. In Step Two, speaking works in the present to attempt to create change. When this proves inconsequential, the Unmoving Mind chooses to hold back words. The transition from speech to silence, from present to future, and from action to anticipation transfers momentum from the Warrior's spontaneous activity to the Hermit's posture of acceptance based on impartiality and equality.

Reticence helps buy time as you assess the impact of challenges and allow for a remedy already initiated by Daijobu to be enacted. During a hiatus in speaking, you can judge the cause of a miscommunication. Without seeming uncooperative or resistant, you can wait until you are prepared to respond decisively. Silence also provides a chance to accumulate knowledge and build support for your cause.

According to an Art of War stratagem that is often cited in Zen writings,

- *Lure the tiger from the hills.*

Do not try to enter into a rival's bastion of strength. By maintaining silence, you compel them to come out of the lair and into the open realm on an even playing field where titles and status are cast aside.

Sometimes the wisest choice is to stay put. Every day on my way to work I have to drive through a complex intersection. Exiting the highway, I must immediately cut across two lanes of traffic that are converging onto an entrance to the same highway that is just a quarter mile past the exit. There is a natural impulse to make for the far lane right through the rush-hour traffic without waiting for the light to stop the oncoming cars. There are accidents small and large nearly every week because someone was unable to wait it out. I have had to develop an instinct that restrains the reflex to succumb to impatience or to the waiting cars honking behind me. That's an example of maintaining a balanced and circumspect outlook.

The kind of waiting in Step Three based on self-control is fundamentally different from the "wait to see if channels will work" approach outlined in Step One, which emphasizes external mechanisms. That is because silence does not simply mean not speaking, just as yielding does not mean inactivity. This third stage of the Encounter sequence builds on the paradox that retreat is attack and losing is winning. The Unmoving Mind accomplishes more by doing and saying less. As Lao Tzu says of the doctrine of "non-action" in the *Tao Te Ching,*

- *The Way does not take action, yet nothing is left undone.*

Cryptic, ambiguous or paradoxical expressions may convey volumes. An oracular or Sphinx-like posture gives others a chance to use their imagination. According to another Taoist saying,

- *Images are based on ideas, and when you get the idea you can forget about the image. Words express images, and when you picture the image you can forget about the words.*

The inspiration for speaking comes from thoughts. However much is spoken will never be able to convey everything you think and feel. But some form of communication is always taking place even when you are not speaking. Like mime or sign language, silence communicates through movements and other actions. You cannot help but telegraph attitudes through gestures and body language. Composer John Cage said there is no such thing as true silence because you can always hear your heartbeat or the hum of the heater or the tick of a clock. A message is perpetually coming across.

An example of body language that communicated more effectively than speaking is seen in John Kennedy's performance in the first-ever, televised presidential debate with Richard Nixon in 1960. Radio listeners gave a slight edge to Nixon, but the TV audience was overwhelmingly sure that Kennedy won the debate. In contrast to his nervous, sickly looking opponent, Kennedy appeared supremely confident. No questions or barbs could shake his appearance of composure. That was the first of four debates, and while everyone remembers vividly the outcome, nobody has any recollection of the next three sessions that took place after the initial impression was set.

A similar illustration appears in the film *The Hustler*, in which Minnesota Fats, played by Jackie Gleason, defeats the brash young pool shark played by Paul Newman. At first Newman is beating the pants off of Fats. He takes a break, relaxing and drinking, while Fats spends the time cleaning up and preparing himself mentally for the contest. Fats returns fresh, focused, and fighting strong. He quickly regains momentum and whips the fatigued challenger, despite Newman's empty taunts.

Once, Senpai was counting on two junior colleagues for major assistance with a project. Both of them were already stretched thin in their schedules. Their abilities were similar, but they had nearly opposite ways of dealing with him. One gave assurances that he would always be available to help until the project reached completion. In the end, however, he had very little time to spare, although Senpai felt clear that the colleague's intention was not impure. The other never said a word about prospects and seemed aloof, but in the end did come through to a greater extent. It was a case of action speaking louder than words. Yet, there was no simple dichotomy here between helpfulness and uselessness. The first colleague's quiet assurances were a comfort and psychological boost that kept the buzz going in Senpai's mind, at least, at times when the second person was not forthcoming. Each of the colleagues contributed in their own unique way to the eventual accomplishment of the task.

On any particular occasion, you must seek to discern whether silence reflects mute unknowingness or is a lion's roar ready to express a full awareness that is being held back until the time is right to have maximum effect. Sometimes reticence may appear disingenuous or duplicitous when eluding an inquiry, avoiding a commitment, or punishing someone with the "silent treatment." A withdrawn silence may reflect emotional agitation.

There are times when you may refuse or be unable to speak, not out of empty-headedness but because you have too much to say or have a tape-loop running in your mind repeating words that would not be appropriate. For example, if you are anxious and your friend senses something by the look on your face and asks what is wrong, you are likely to say simply,

- *Nothing.*

This means there is no one single thing wrong but too much to even begin trying to explain it. Is this kind of nothingness meaningful? This is like the joke in which a girl complains that she doesn't like Swiss cheese because of the holes and her mother tells her, "Leave the holes on the plate and just eat the cheese."

Some forms of purposeful silence are more expressive than words because they stem from the inner wisdom of the Hermit. I once saw the great blues guitarist B. B. King fire off an incredible riff then stop in midstream to play "air guitar." The silence of this moment made a thunderous roar that, judging from the audience's response, seemed to outshine the audible notes played before and after. Perhaps that is why Bill Evans said that the magic of John Coltrane's music was more than a matter of musical notes coaxed from a physical instrument. The music spoke right to the heart on an unmediated level beyond the distinction between sound and silence.

The Zen notion of "intuitive communication from mind to mind" is not the supernatural ability to read minds or transmit thoughts but rather the achievement of insight based on mutual understanding. According to a parable, the Buddha goes to spread the Dharma on a distant planet where the inhabitants have such an advanced degree of spiritual insight that he doesn't need to utter a sound while teaching. Eye contact and gestures alone are sufficient to convey doctrines. When he returns to planet Earth, the Buddha realizes that humans fail to heed the teaching because they are pigheaded and stubborn in their attachments. He must continually adjust and adapt both words and silence in different ways tailored to the understanding of his followers, even if this involves ambiguity or contradiction. As the Zen poet Ryokan says,

- *When you realize that my poems are not really poems, then we can sit down and discuss poetry.*

As opposed to reticence that is the result of feeling stuck and not knowing what to say, silence based on choice lets you remain ambiguous in a creative way until you see how circumstances unfold. The building of bridges, alliances, and consensus with helpful colleagues must gird under being silent, so that the over-all force of what is said and left unsaid is maximized. This actually enhances the effectiveness of Daijobu Diplomacy because what others say in your absence can do more to advance the cause than what you say about yourself. The integrity of ideas supported by a network of cultivated alliances wins the day. It can be better for a well-positioned colleague to serve as your advocate than for you to press your own case.

True silence reflects mastery of knowing when and what to say and not to say. Senpai was trying to sell a project and the client asked for a report on productivity figures up to that point. He presented a detailed, itemized account, demonstrating that he was fully prepared for the query. But even though the overall picture was on the rosy side, when the specs were scrutinized, a subtle pattern of declining productivity was exposed. The client's early enthusiasm faded like the dew on a late summer blossom and he quickly and quietly backed off. When pressed for an explanation, the client gave this advice: show the rosy picture but do not disclose details that may undermine prospects. The structure of negotiations is fluid and is being determined by what is or is not expressed.

HOLDING THE FLY-WHISK WHILE
FACING THE POINT OF NO RETURN

What happens when both speaking and silence fail to challenge the status quo or to bring about an appropriate change in structure? The last refuge of a hierarchical organization is to assert dominance by evoking power through a symbol of authority (rather than verbiage). Kuei-shan raising the fly-whisk is a classic example of the invocation of such a symbol, which has the effect of pulling rank on the upstart Te-shan. In another koan case, a master of one school of Zen holds up his fly-whisk before a visitor who represents a different sect and asks,

- *Do they have anything like this where you come from?*

However, in the final analysis, all symbols, like words in Step Two, prove themselves to be hollow shells whose claim to commanding respect depends entirely on the integrity of the person using them.

At a committee meeting where you are scheduled to present a report summarizing your ideas for launching an important project, a challenge is likely to come from both sides. It stems from those who have been waiting forever for innovation and feel that the changes recommended are inadequate and from those who will resist any departure from what is considered the norm. The one thing both sides agree on is to question your role and challenge the basis of your authority. You realize your position could be undermined at any moment depending on whether you handle a crisis of uncertainty as an opportunity for growth or a time to get rigid. When you stretch a rubber band, the opening widens but eventually it will break.

One person emerges as spokesman for the challenge and waves a copy of your report in front of the whole group while saying, "Isn't this old wine in new bottles?" The question is not so much about the document in their hands as it is about who really holds power, and whether you can drive your point home despite the objections coming from opposite angles. At this stage, you turn to a member of the committee managing the budget, and ask how much of the funds could be committed to the project. He has been sitting back and watching, and now retorts, "What if there was nothing? Can't we accomplish almost all of your proposals without committing new resources?" You could then try to give your approach even more of a buzz by volunteering to take on additional responsibility to generate funds or just put a rather abrupt end to your portion of the meeting with a shrug and the comment, "We'll see."

Ideally, this shrug is done not to show offhanded indifference but to **Hold the Thought**, or refrain from stating what is clear to everyone and need not be spoken, that if the committee is brought down by turf battles and fails to accomplish its goals, there will be more of a problem than anyone wants to see. At this juncture, you might consider leaping into anti-structure by grabbing the papers that have been used to taunt, which are a product of your work after all, or simply walking away from the table. However, the groundwork for such a dramatic, irreverent gesture needs to be laid by one more preliminary step, so you have come prepared with an updated, more comprehensive and fully documented version of the report that you pull out of your briefcase. This has all the facts and figures required to prove and disprove the contested points, and jaws drop in an admiring silence.

At the decisive moment, this symbol functions like a yellow light that signals for all to slow down the pace of the meeting. This pause in activity has a dynamic quality in allowing for a re-channeling of the energy circulating in the room. However, the symbol, or counter-symbol, is useful and productive only so long as it promotes dialogue and leads to a mutually beneficial result. If the spokesperson for the objections has one item in his hands (even if it means defacing a symbol you generated) while you have another, you are left with a clash of empty symbols waved back and forth.

This exchange featuring two useless sets of physical materials leaves basic issues unexamined and unresolved. The futility of using icons of authority is revealed in the limitation of symbols representing power that is in turn based on the emptiness at the root of all structures. In recognizing this, you will be led to pursue genuine power by taking the leap in Step Four into the realm of anti-structure.

Often, something that is supposed to convey a greater sense of power than what actually is thereby functioning as a meaningful symbol of authority is exposed as nothing more than a three-dimensional object. The philosopher Kierkegaard tells a story of a man, feeling distraught and desperate, who prowls the streets late at night and discovers to his delight a shop with a sign announcing, "Philosophy Done Here." He goes toward the entrance and then in the dark sees that it is merely a store selling signs. This demonstrates the lesson that sometimes what you take to be a tool of communication turns out to be simply one more meaningless object.

One time Senpai started managing a unit that had a low level of productivity in an important sector. The quotient was actually in single digits, and he worked hard to double the figure within six months. His immediate supervisor was proud of the team's efforts. Then they discovered that while they were reporting a total figure of 17, the official records had them down for only 12. It was explained that the VP's office had a stricter method of accounting. But when Senpai recalculated using this other method he still came up with the seemingly impressive number of 15.

Senpai prepared a beautiful document with all the bells and whistles and made an appointment upstairs. As he and his supervisor started to make their argument, they found the VP was a step ahead and caught them off guard by saying,

- *Whether you have a quotient of 17 or 12 or 15 doesn't really matter much, because we are only paying attention to units with the potential to reach 50.*

Therefore, the beautifully designed report was yet another dispensable symbol in a world of cast-asides and throwaways. Babe Ruth could have waved his finger all he wanted that famous day, but if he had not actually hit a home run straight out to dead center it would have been a mockery.

This was a time when Senpai should have been better prepared, based on dynamic activity and genuine accomplishment, to make a dramatic statement that threw away the numbers and wiped the slate clean. As the Wesley Snipes character in *Rising Sun* says in frustration to fellow detective Sean Connery, who has been mentoring what he calls his Kohai (junior colleague) on how to "negotiate" with the Japanese during a homicide investigation,

- *Senpai. Apple pie. Or whatever you want me to call you.*

CHAPTER EIGHT

Coming from Nowhere
to Somewhere

Step 4

ENTERING THE REALM OF
ANTI-STRUCTURE
(Knowing)

THE AIM OF SILENCE in Step Three is to reflect logically on emotional reactions before putting forth a view. Silence helps contain the fire and lets it burn slowly to help discover what is real and what is illusory. Bringing a crisis to a head clarifies where things stand and determines whether a stronger response is needed. But what happens when the unstoppable drive of ambition meets head on with the immovable strength of the fly-whisk?

Logic provides a check and balance for emotion, but reason has its own shortcomings and when the rational mind runs its course it is necessary to turn to intuition. Once the full resources of speaking and not speaking, as well as symbols of authority, have all been tried without success, then and only then do you bring into play the last resort of anti-structural behavior demonstrating typical Zen qualities of spontaneity, irreverence, and contradiction. Anti-structure does not rely on speaking but is also not just a matter of staying silent. The conventions of hierarchy and organizational procedures are cast aside but are by no means disdained or disrespected. This transforms the conventional injunction of "think before you speak" into,

- *Before thinking or speaking awaken the Unmoving Mind, and then you can either think or speak more effectively.*

When Senpai was asked to give "one word of Zen," a traditional phrase referring to a distillation of the path, he would often say,

- *Jump!*

Quoting from a koan case in which this terse command is given as the answer to the question, "What do you do after you climb to the top of a 100-foot pole?" One time he was pressed for a further explanation and he grunted,

- *Don't jump!*

Was Senpai being deliberately arbitrary or merely jocular? The fear was that he might be starting to resemble one of those unhelpful Zen teachers described by Yukio Mishima:

- *Then, of course, there is the type of Zen priest who will instantly hand down his arbitrary decision on anything that is discussed, but who will be careful to phrase his reply in such a way that it can be taken to mean two opposite things.*

Senpai's oblique style of discourse meant that there comes a point when neither more communication nor turning away will solve the problem, or when conventional behavior has exhausted its path yet any alternative risks alienating friend and foe alike. At that moment, you must make a split-second decision whether to jump or not to jump. It is impossible to decide beforehand which option will be preferable, as both have pros and cons relative to the particular context, but your choice determines whether you gain or lose heaven.

The leap from structure to anti-structure is a technique for solving otherwise intractable problems. This delicate maneuver must be approached carefully. Anti-structural words or deeds are only effective in creating authority and fielding a challenge when you stay aligned with the principle of fairness. Outrageous behavior is useful if it is based on substance and it is clear you have done everything possible before resorting to strangeness. Impermissible motives include wanting to denigrate others or looking for individual credit rather than giving priority to teamwork and self-sacrifice.

There are several essential elements of anti-structure. First, the progression of the four steps has a dialectical quality. The steps all have the capacity to solve the problem. But if a step plays out and eventually collapses on its own, this signals that the issue is more deep seated and leads to the next stage. Each stage corrects its predecessor, yet also reveals a shortcoming or flaw that contains the seeds of its remedial successor.

Once you recognize a difficulty or obstacle as a source of suffering, it is necessary to try to correct the condition by first going through procedures. Start by returning to the root condition and beginning the remedial process from that vantage point, without skipping over stages. Be careful not to jump around in an undisciplined way without regard to sequence—for example, keeping silent before speaking or experimenting with anti-structure prior to working within structure—as this will compound rather than alleviate the core difficulty. Do not try to push ahead by forcing a new stage before it is necessary or unless you are ready for it, but don't cling to a stage after it has clearly become a dead issue.

A second element exhibited by Te-shan's reentering the Dharma Hall is the need for a face-to-face meeting to complete the Encounter. I remember having a car that was always on the fritz and calling my friend, who was a mechanic, with endless questions, but I always acted like I was too busy to bring it in, partly to benefit from the free advice. Finally, out of frustration, he asked, "When you're sick, do you talk endlessly to the doctor on the phone, or do you go into his office?"

Senpai once had a disciple who seemed to be avoiding him. On a previous project, she had done a brilliant job that earned his admiration. But he had been disappointed in her recent performance. When she saw that Senpai was trying to promote a colleague who had less experience, the disciple wanted to make her own case known. However, she complained to everyone else but Senpai. He understood that on some level she was aware that she had no moral authority to insist on a raise or claim unfair treatment. If she had shown up in his office to confront him, he would have been happy to explain that her recent work had been far from effective. She knew she was not ready for the Encounter. Her realization that she did not want to hear this message turned into a penitent moment that motivated her to go back to Senpai and have an in-depth discussion on how to improve productivity without regard for reward. In the end her renewed efforts were noted and the raise was granted.

A third element of anti-structure is that the intuition of Zen masters is generally expressed in unpredictable behavior, such as by reacting to the same situation in opposite ways or to opposite situations in the same way. At other times, this calls for role reversals, in which disciples strike or slap their masters. Other techniques include absurdity and humor, paradoxes and nonsequiturs, as well as nonverbal or demonstrative gestures, such as jumping from poles, cutting off limbs, burning sutras, or tossing away sacred objects. These methods are invoked not as a show of eccentricity as an end in itself, but with a particular effect in mind, and should be cast aside abruptly as soon as the desired result has been achieved.

In some koan cases, the master displays contradictory or ever-shifting responses to the same behavior, for example, answering variously yes, no, or maybe to the same question. Sometimes, the pattern is reversed, as when Chao-chou responds with "Go have a cup of tea" to all the diverse queries he receives. When he was asked why he always instructed in the same way, Chao-chou smilingly told the inquirer,

- *Go have a cup of tea.*

Saying Goodbye to Water Pitchers, Everywhere

Zen masters repeatedly show that humor and irony, when used without sarcasm or condescension, can disarm possible rivals and adversaries and create compromise by allowing you to say things you could not express otherwise. In a contemporary non-Zen example, Judge Griffen Bell, who was not used to the political scene, was a surprise appointee to the post of attorney general in the Carter administration. He was an outsider at a time when the FBI, now under his jurisdiction, was increasingly coming under scrutiny and attack for being too politicized. At a press conference, the new AG-designate was bombarded with questions from reporters. Was he depressed over the lack of morale at the Bureau, or impressed with the magnitude of his authority? Did he know if any evidence implicating members of the FBI had been suppressed by the previous administration? Were the feds guilty of the repression of human rights, as many claimed? The nominee stood there calmly and said,

- *Depressed? Impressed? Suppressed? Repressed? Let's just say, I'm pressed!*

Of course, the sly humor showed that he wasn't going to be dragged down by the legacy he had inherited (although he would soon be driven from office for other reasons, proving again, that talk is cheap and actions do speak louder).

A meeting between Senpai and several middle-aged, middle-level managers provides another example of spontaneous humor. Things had become quite tense. Hanging in the air was the implication that Senpai was the stubborn, incorrigible one. He, on the other hand, felt confident that while sticking to principles, when the time came, he would be able to show that he was willing to yield. Still, he was pushing maybe too hard for a clear resolution by the end of the day, which was what his supervisor was expecting. Somehow the conversation turned to a senior colleague who, though long retired, was still active in certain affairs. One person said how remarkable it was that "she was 80 but looked and acted not a day over 50." Senpai shot back,

- *And we're all 50, yet we look and act not a day younger than 80.*

This rather outrageous remark might have upset someone, but it turned out to be just the right kind of icebreaker. It drew attention to the fact that they weren't getting anywhere. The conversation could then open up and move forward to a productive conclusion.

One time a friend told Senpai that her supervisors acted very enthusiastic about her projects but never really came through with the support promised. She wasn't sure whether they simply lacked resources and were doing their best with smoke and mirrors. How could she be sure they really stood behind her to the extent they led her to believe? During a negotiation session, the supervisors once again promised additional support, but when she analyzed the trade-offs involved, it hardly seemed worth the trouble. Then they invoked the idea that it would be a matter of "robbing from Peter to pay Paul."

Senpai's friend tried to stay focused on the question, Were they sincere or disingenuous? She said, "This is the first time you've talked about playing the Peter-Paul game," to which they replied, "We always talk about it." She told them,

- *Maybe this is the first time I've heard you admit to it.*

Being open about what is normally concealed had the effect of putting everyone at ease and opening up the purse strings just enough that she came away from the meeting satisfied with the response.

In a courtroom show on TV, an unorthodox lawyer played by a young Peter Falk came into a boardroom meeting. His peers were conducting a review of the eccentric behavior that accompanied his tremendously effective though unconventional and idiosyncratic legal counsel. Was he a menace to the profession? The Falk character was of course disheveled and wore a very loud tie loosened at an open collar. When the head of the inquiry commented facetiously, "I like your tie," Falk responded by taking the tie off and tossing it across on the conference table and saying,

- *You like it?... Here, it's yours.*

Take it or leave it was the message of the day.

Unraveling Scrolls and Twirling Bats

The Unmoving Mind deals with shifting alliances and surprising developments by seeing clearly and objectively the unfolding of things as they are and giving priority to the most productive tasks. News that there is a problem in the workplace may create an opportunity for action and advancement. If you can help solve problems that others cause, you build up credentials that help prepare for a time when you must take a bolder, Step Four-type of move by "Creating a problem to solve a problem."

The first stage of Senpai's training of junior colleagues to prime them for this maneuver was based on Elevation. He explained how to cast aside ego and ascend by stepping back from the world of discord and abandon thoughts of winning or losing, living or dying, as well as the "nothing to fear but fear itself" syndrome. Because you show yourself willing to accept defeat and death, adversaries are disarmed and the desired results of victory and life are gained.

Senpai's mentoring was tested when he assigned one of his trainees to make an all-important presentation before an uncompromising, "always demand the best," advisory board. This presentation would determine the fate of a project that was crucial to the advancement of the whole unit. He decided, somewhat controversially, that this was an opportune time to put the spotlight on his main disciple. She had been assisting him for months in readying the report and knew the material better than he. She was eager to prove herself, but we all knew of a potentially fatal weakness. It seemed problematic to push her forward, but Senpai's plan was precisely to heighten the challenge in order to lead to a more complete result.

The disciple had come to the group after being trained in a methodology based on statistical analysis of quantifiable data. While she did an outstanding job with subtle analytic work, this was very much at odds with the humanist method favored by a powerful member of the board. The board member felt that numbers could never tell the whole story and when given the chance sermonized eloquently about the importance of recognizing quality over the quantifiable. The two methods of interpretation worked with data acquired during extensive interviews in the field. Once this raw data is taken back to the office for examination, it could be interpreted in much the same way by both approaches. The statistical method favored a spreadsheet-generating mathematical model, and the humanist approach highlighted anecdotes evoking human interest.

At a critical juncture in an analysis, the results of the respective methods might appear to part ways and lead to different conclusions. Senpai was skilled at bridging that gap, calling up anecdotes from his mental archives to flesh out the numbers and harmonize the respective conclusions. He knew how to find common ground, how to make left wing and right wing fly together.

For his disciple, the challenge was to avoid getting trapped by the classic dichotomy between number crunching and concepts.

She was prone to get flustered down the stretch of a grueling interrogation, especially if hostile questions kept coming at high speed. Forced to step out of her normal style, she might not be able to resist the opportunity to speak too much and undermine herself with her own words. The rest of the team, it was feared, would be forced to sit idly by while the fortunes of the unit went down the tubes.

Whoever presented the report would have to field questions without allowing methodological discrepancies to emerge as an Achilles heel. The debate about methodology could take on a life of its own and obscure the underlying strength in the content of the report. Senpai himself had a ton of experience and worked comfortably in both methodological worlds. We fully expected that in the end he would come to his senses and grab the reins for the presentation. There was too much at stake going into this meeting, and the only way to fend off the skeptical board member and avoid a fiasco would be to have Senpai on the firing line. But that would not be a very good example of "Creating a problem to solve a problem."

Prior to the big event, Senpai held a private meeting and reassured the disciple that he had full confidence in her ability, which lifted her spirits. He prepared her to expect the interview with the board to come down to a single all-encompassing Moment when every bit of planning would have to be thrown out the window as the light of the sun poured brilliantly in.

Senpai explained that the Unmoving Mind is both active in articulating a vision for change and yielding in accepting the need for open-ended decision making. The Hermit's way gives you the assuredness to be immune to attack and indifferent to any unfair or unfounded critique, so that you can walk away from conflict with an indifferent attitude. The uncaring quality of the Mind is empty of insistence or expectation. Uncaring, unlike ordinary doubt, is not a matter of giving up out of fatigue, exhaustion, or feeling demoralized because the situation is hopeless and cannot be remedied. It means unlearning bad habits to allow a new kind of instinct to open up.

A jazz conductor once told his musicians to study the score till they knew every note backwards and forwards and then,

- *Just forget the chart and play!*

Senpai's disciple needed to cast aside the distractions of fear and inflated hopes and allow the Unmoving Mind to flow freely as a unity of thinking and speaking in a new form of improvisation. At the crucial Moment she would "play her music" freely. But she had to exercise supreme patience while waiting for that tiny instant to arrive.

Unraveling the Scroll or Shaking out the Quilt is an exercise that integrates the Hermit's overview, which yields to the interconnectedness of all perspectives, with the Warrior's ability to engage appropriately at the precise Moment. Suppose you have a scroll that is rolled up or a quilt that has been thrown in the corner of the closet. You try to decipher the scroll from start to finish. The way a scroll is ordinarily read, you only see one portion at a time and you have to take the unusual and somewhat cumbersome or arduous step of unrolling it all the way to see the big picture. If you open the scroll part way you can only read a portion of the narrative without seeing what comes before or after. Picking up the rumpled quilt, it seems too short. But when you allow the scroll to unfold or the quilt to be flattened out, everything that was there all along becomes apparent and you can decipher or utilize each and every minute detail.

Senpai's disciple needed to read from the metaphorical scroll laid out properly, so that she could see the whole picture from the beginning to the end. She would be prepared and braced not to overreact to the questioner's prodding, which would be one of the scroll's wrinkles that needed to be unraveled. Senpai instructed her to let the board members do their thing, and when necessary—and only then—he would be sure to deflect the attack and save the presentation. But at first he had to appear aloof and indifferent, as if he were only a spectator sitting on the sidelines, so as to enhance his objectivity and clarity. The success of his involvement depended on how well the disciple kept her poise and balance during the rough spots, which were sure to come. This would enable him to identify the flaw in the questioner's strategy and judge the right time for leaping into the fray.

Takuan Soho describes how the Zen outlook functions when it reenters the world of everyday activity:

- *Where to set the mind?...If you set your mind on an opponent's actions, you have your mind taken up by the opponent's actions....If you set your mind on your own sword, you have your mind taken up by your own sword. The point is that there is nowhere at all to set the mind, which is what gives you the freedom to act...*

By not allowing itself to become fixed, the Unmoving Mind masters the art of anticipating the next move in order to select appropriate action or inaction.

Some people talk about foreseeing the future through visualizing events that may take place. There are those who look for lightning to strike, while others consult soothsayers or analyze their dreams. Zen teaches that timing is a state of mind. I remember sitting in a park with some friends. Another member of our group walked by, slow as molasses, stepping very deliberately, first one foot and then the other. We called out for him to come over and join our chat:

- *"Can't do it," he shook his head, "I'm in too much of a hurry."*

While the world often puts pressure on you to,

- *Hurry up and waste time,*

the message of Zen is to seize the moment by,

- *Striking quickly and then waiting (or vice versa).*

The Zen Mind intuitively tracks developments based on past experience in order to stay steps ahead of the competition. A heightened sense of anticipation makes you aware that every process is bound by an endpoint or deadline. Because Zen spontaneity allows you to be aware of how events occurring midway through a process may help determine the outcome, you can continuously rethink and adjust plans based on lessons being learned. You play a game with one eye on the clock, calculating what should be the influence on current strategies of the final moments yet to come, and how what is done or not done now will likely turn out.

Sometimes you adopt the role of the tortoise in undertaking methodical planning, and at other times, the hare in you is bounding forward on the spur of the moment. Either way, you will never know for sure how what you did not do would have turned out if only you had done it.

Then there are the Silky Sullivan opportunities. Silky Sullivan, one of the most beloved race horses in history, won several contests in 1958, including the Santa Anita Derby. At first he conceded a huge lead to his rivals as he hung at the very end of the pack, as much as 30 lengths behind the other horses. Then, ready to make his move, he began a ferocious charge that was victorious at the finish line. That day, the horse won a race and a corner in Zen heaven. (In the interest of full disclosure, I must admit that the technique failed Silky in the all-important Kentucky Derby. TV coverage of the Derby that year featured a split image, with Silky Sullivan the favorite shown in a corner of the screen because he was not even close enough for the camera to capture him in the same shot with the pack. In that race, he did not show, finishing 20 lengths behind the winner, Tim Tan. There is a Zen lesson here as well, in that you can't expect the same approach to win every time.)

Senpai prepared his disciple for hitting the Silky Sullivan stride at the right instant. Timing would mean everything. He told her that, at the meeting, a Moment would come when the skeptic would disparage the statistical method and through a series of

A close-up of Silky Sullivan above, and a shot of his late dash at Santa Anita below

probing questions would tempt her to commit to a particular view she would not be comfortable with. This would leave her without room for retreat, and would likely doom the entire project.

He advised the disciple to maintain utmost control and patience. When challenged, do not take it personally. Respond with the assumption that when the dust settles and the limits of egotistical methods are exposed, it is the most genuinely constructive agenda that will prevail. She should resist the questioner's effort to corner her, but without clamming up and appearing unprepared or overreacting and saying things that might reveal a fatal weakness. Senpai assured her that by staying composed she would buy him the time to figure out how best to address and disarm the board member.

The meeting unfolded as expected. The adversary had proceeded unswervingly down a path of logical and penetrating queries. The disciple became a bit unsettled and started to lose her balance. Senpai's opportunity came when the overconfident adversary asked just one too many questions, saying,

- *Why doesn't your model ever deal with the actual concerns of real people?*

Senpai leapt in,

- *I've been following your line of reasoning and am left wondering, are you more interested in the actual concerns of real people or in arguing over methods for dealing with them?*

Then he briefly but eloquently explained how the disciple's numbers addressed more than satisfactorily all of the issues the board member had raised. Case closed. A new suite of offices and all the perks you could want were on the way. The character played by Ricky Jay in the film *Heist* might have been talking about Senpai when he said of the Gene Hackman role,

- *My m—f— is so cool, when sheep can't sleep, they count him.*

The story of Senpai's finesse calls to mind the savvy and skill of Willie Stargell, the star hitter who led the Pittsburgh Pirates to World Series victory in 1979. Stargell was a big guy and they used to say the bat looked like a toothpick in his hands. During a key at-bat late in a game at the height of the pennant race the radio announcer would say, "Stargell's twirling the toothpick." If the announcer said it one time it was no big deal, but when they repeated it a second or third time you knew it was going to be a home run derby. Stargell was seeing his pitch coming down the pike.

Consider why the bat became like a toothpick for Willie Stargell. The size or shape of the wood in the batter's hand never changed a bit. What did change was Stargell's demeanor, which, with the game on the line, expressed a new power and authority. He appeared to be twirling a toothpick because the bat had become a tool in his hands that he completely controlled. He was the master of the bat as an instrument, rather than vice versa. And when he slammed a home run (like any batter), he dropped the tool of hitting as he circled the bases.

According to an ancient legend, Zen Buddhism originated when Sakyamuni Buddha preached a nonverbal sermon simply by **twirling a flower** in his hands and smiling. One person in the assembly, the venerable Mahakasyapa, understood the meaning and gained an awakening that was transmitted to later generations. What insight did Mahakasyapa receive that day by seeing a gleam in Sakyamuni's eye? Many interpretations focus on the role of silence as key to this primal event, but others emphasize the act of twirling the flower.

The term "twirling" came to be used in Zen to refer to a master reflecting on a koan case by turning it over in his mind and examining its significance from every possible angle. Each interpretation is considered carefully and there is no commitment to or insistence on a particular view, leaving this to be decided by the reader or disciple. However, the records of Zen koans generally do not transcribe the full set of deliberations but instead capture brief, dramatic, and enigmatic comments proffered by the masters. This heightens the sense of mystery of Zen sayings. The point is that you gain control by making use of the koan. The koan does not control you.

The same rule applies to the elements of Zen discipline. The ways of the Hermit and Warrior seen in terms of the process of EPA help develop self-control as well as a confident and cooperative attitude. Once the task is completed, it is important to dispense with the means that were used to achieve the purpose. You order using a menu but then eat the food and set the menu aside. You gather the fish and cast aside the net. Once the light is on, you forget about the switch. To paraphrase a Zen saying,

- *A Mind that is enlightened turns the wheel of the law, and the Mind that is not enlightened is turned by the wheel.*

Or as Taoist philosopher Chuang tzu says,

- *There are those who use many words and those who use no words. Let me meet a man of no words, so that I can sit down over a cup of tea and have a few words with him.*

FULL-COURT GAME AS
THE WAY OF TEAMWORK

White Collar Zen can be summed up as the unity of two forces. One force associated with Beat Zen is **Singularity**, or all the unique creativity that you can summon, even if seemingly eccentric and anomalous, to express your individual talent. Each snowflake has a distinctive design.

The second force, associated with Square Zen, is **Solidarity**. Inspiring teamwork brings out the talent in colleagues who may otherwise remain recalcitrant and mired in mediocrity. More than individual effort is needed to prevail in an Encounter. Phil Jackson's *Sacred Hoops: Spiritual Lessons of a Hardwood Warrior* applies this Zen principle to the professional basketball arena with the distinctive strategy of a "**Full-Court Game,**" which he calls the "Tao of basketball," or "five-man tai-chi." Jackson, one of the most successful coaches in the history of the sport, who is consistently referred to as the "Zen master of basketball" by the media, coached superstar Michael Jordan at the peak of his career. Sportscasters used to say of Jordan,

- *He controls the whole court by having the knack of coming from nowhere to somewhere.*

He starts away from the ball on the far side of the court and spontaneously, almost without being noticed, surfaces in the heat of the action for a crucial pass, score, or rebound that turns the tide of the game.

Jackson used Zen insight to develop techniques that utilized the best skills of all the players and kept the ball moving around the entire court. Teamwork, based on dynamic, interactive offensive and defensive strategies, leads to victory. His method enabled his players to defeat both conventional man-to-man and zone coverages by catching opponents flatfooted and unprepared. With Jordan on his side, Jackson might have won championships without Zen. But it would have been easy for Jordan's dominance to eclipse the talents of his teammates. It is fascinating to see how strategies based on the Unmoving Mind set the stage for the superstar to display exceptional mastery while integrating his strengths with those of the rest of the team.

The Full-Court Game is a comprehensive and integrative approach that values cooperation and mutuality over individualism, which means playing with all your wits and skills at each stage and on every level, perpetually setting strategy in motion without any apparent effort. All participants are enabled to rise to the occasion with their best performance. The Full-Court Game is different from the more customary "full-court press," a technique that guards opponents in the backcourt as they are bringing up the ball. This strenuous and fatiguing maneuver can be effective in breaking the momentum of the game, but should be held in reserve as a technique of last resort used only in a time of desperation.

Two levels of Encounter are taking place in a Full-Court Game. In the first, within the inner group—between Jordan and teammates— a star acts as a supportive Buddha, bringing out the best in players who normally exhibit more pedestrian skills. The five players yield Hermit-like to their respective potentials and limits and find harmony and a new sense of confidence along with the courage to act. Bill Walton, an outstanding basketball player of the 1970s, was the superstar who single-handedly carried the dark horse Portland Trailblazers to a championship. The key to the Trailblazers' success was Walton's thoroughly selfless, "We, not me" teamwork. When asked how Walton accomplished so much, a commentator said,

- *By never letting mediocrity enter into his game, even for a single play, he brings out greatness in teammates and elevates players who otherwise would probably remain mediocre.*

The second level of Encounter takes place between the two teams. Jackson's strategies leave the opposition defenseless. If the other team puts multiple defenders on Jordan, he spontaneously dishes off for an assist. If they go to man-to-man coverage, he exploits the weakness of the defender, whether tall or short, swift or plodding. In both cases, Jordan & Co. effectively utilize the conceptual space of the court, which complements and enhances the players' individual talents and teamwork. In the early days of pro football, the great quarterback Sammy Baugh once said that if his team was protecting the passer properly he could play his position "wearing a tuxedo." This is like Chuang Tzu's comment that a Taoist butcher never needs to sharpen his knife because he knows how to cut through the material.

The process of attaining greatness in self and others by combining the forces of Singularity and Solidarity is addressed in a Confucian parable. A man steals the sheep of his neighbor, and it is his eldest son who learns of the crime and helps his father rectify the wrong he has done. A contemporary analogy might be a supervisor who has neglected to complete the final report of an important project while a junior associate, who has been collecting and organizing the data, becomes aware of the omission. This creates a quandary for the junior person, who has been doing his job well, even though the supervisor is the one at fault. How do you get the supervisor to acknowledge his failure and promptly correct it? If the associate were to report the lapse to someone higher in the organization it would be a breach of basic protocol, but doing nothing at all may cause the unit, including his own position, to collapse.

There are two other options. One is to speak behind the scenes with a more senior figure, who would be able to apply pressure to the supervisor. But this must be done without appearing to go behind the supervisor's back. The other choice is for the junior person to take it upon himself to complete the report, thereby setting an example the supervisor will eventually follow. The challenge is to do this in an uplifting rather than humiliating way.

By taking the second option (only after having explored the sequence of four steps), the associate has broken through the formidable invisible barriers of hierarchical status and rank. This is done without going against the grain, but rather by elevating the ideals of institutional structure. If greatness is genuine, then it has its own effect and there is no need to talk about or proclaim it for personal credit.

In order to induce others to be great, you have to be responsible for becoming great yourself, showing them the way. As Confucius says, there is a reciprocal process of establishing merit:

- *The way to be great is to make others great. It is the greatness of others that makes each of us great.*

Leading by example in a world in which all relations are interdependent and interactive establishes a spiritually "authoritative" position that advances the overall good rather than an "authoritarian" attitude that uses coercion or intimidation. According to a Taoist text,

- *When the wrong person uses the right means the means are used incorrectly, but when the right person uses the wrong means the means are used correctly.*

Everyone is born with the potential to become a leader, but to be elevated into the status of authority on the bureaucratic ladder you need to be supported by those on higher rungs who demonstrate leadership qualities. Whoever has a reputation for excellent accomplishments, sound judgment, reasonable arguments, and impeccable integrity, will be listened to attentively. If you are not occupying a position of greatness, the next best thing is to identify and inspire the support of those who will speak up on your behalf, behind the scenes, in a way that carries much more weight than any amount of self-promotion. As Confucius recommends,

- *The practice of government leadership by means of virtue may be compared with the North Star, around which the multitudinous heavenly bodies revolve while it stays in its place.*

A genuine leader is the first to critique and dismiss the inadequate and to admire and praise junior colleagues who surpass your accomplishments:

- *When it is necessary to lead he leads, and when it is necessary to cooperate he cooperates;*
  When it is necessary to use soft training methods he uses soft training methods, and when it is necessary to be harsh he is harsh.

At the Moment of completing an Encounter, or when you have made mountains mountains once again, Zen teachers say:

- *The sun rises in the east and sets in the west;*

- *The rooster crows at the break of dawn,* and

- *A leap year comes every one in four.*

Another Zen phrase evokes the serenity of natural beauty, of perceiving reality in all its diverse manifestations blissfully free of bias or partial judgment:

- *Willows are green, flowers are red.*

Epilogue: Guaranteed Success, But What to do with Failure

A successful Encounter is intended to have a continually renewable, long-term effect, transforming a person who is locked into a position of conflict into a reliable ally and pillar of support. Senpai would be the last to claim that an Encounter could solve every problem and the first to admit this approach did not have all the answers. He understood the Dylan lyric, "There's no success like failure." Any time you succeed you also fall short. After a major achievement, you may expect a reward of comparable proportions but it will be limited because successes are not permanent and there will always be challenges. He also realized the inverse is often the case: there is no failure like success if you cannot see beyond temporary ups and downs and find a lesson that can inspire you in future endeavors.

There was the time Senpai won a significant contract from an agency and felt he deserved a new office. The far side of the building had floor-to-ceiling windows and a gorgeous river view. Senpai started referring to the offices located there as the "Glass Suite." He may not have coined this usage, but his contribution was to use the Glass Suite as a metaphor for more than an attractive space gained as a reward for making a slam dunk. It meant a whole package of perks and resources put at your creative disposal, including staff, budget, equipment, etc. It did not just imply status and prestige, but concrete acquisitions that would be vital in achieving additional goals.

Senpai's request was greeted with a resounding thud of silence from supervisors, who would not say yes, no, or maybe. As time passed and the system would not budge, he was entering the stage when he needed to produce results while laboring on with the same limited resources he had before the contract, which he thought would bring him Nirvana on earth. Senpai was stymied. He could not tell if the silence reflected resistance by higher levels of management or the reluctance of an individual who was utterly noncommittal when they exchanged greetings briefly at a meeting on an unrelated matter. Was no news in this case good news, and the rewards could be expected to be forthcoming? Or had the request run into a complication that would not soon be resolved? Maybe the matter had not yet been brought before an advisory unit. Or perhaps it was simply considered out of the question and off the table, but nobody had the guts to tell him so.

Senpai, apparently at a peak, was reminded of the sarcastic comment that concludes the Te-shan koan,

- *Sitting amid the weeds on the summit of the solitary mountain peak.*

In the midst of resolving a problem, the seeds of another are rooted and straggly weeds begin to sprout. Writing of the experience of enlightenment, Dogen says,

- *Nevertheless, flowers continue to fall to our dismay and weeds still spring up to our chagrin.*

No one can guess every fork in the road. Zen agrees with Nietzsche that from ignorance or arrogance we are,

- *Human, all too human.*

As advanced in insight and enlightenment as a Satori may be, there are still limitations and constraints:

- *Even a Buddha carries a wooden board over his shoulder.*

If there is a board across the right shoulder and you are called on from the front, left or rear, you can easily see who is there, although you may need to turn your head or upper torso a bit. But if the call comes from the right side, while you may have a partial view a blind spot remains unless you shift your whole body, or move or remove the board.

No matter how good your peripheral vision, there are no exceptions to the rule of obstruction. There is always an angle not understood, a side of the story not heard, or a strand not threaded through the needle. Something is missing in every approach, a skill remains unlearned and a potential unfulfilled, or someone is let down. The silence Senpai now faced, like the mystery surrounding the competition when he was a young researcher, was hidden somewhere on the other side of the **Buddha's board.**

Dogen further explains that inherent constraints cannot be separated from enlightenment. A full understanding of sights and sounds or a clear perception of each sensation is not omniscience:

- *When one side is illumined, the other side is dark.*

You remain bound by the limits of human knowledge, which are like a horizon that creates a natural barrier. Beyond this not-so-imaginary line, you cannot see. According to the image of Shangri-la in *Lost Horizon*, the horizon is "lost" in that you do not see it because you are too busy thinking you can see beyond it.

The aim is to illumine as many sides or perspectives as humanly possible. Zen recognizes, however, that at any given time the proverbial board blocks at least a part of your view. In the *Temple of the Golden Pavilion*, the main character Mizoguchi has two close friends from separate areas of his life. One is tried and tested and true blue. The other is not nearly so trustworthy but someone he has had to rely on out of necessity. In Mizoguchi's mind they are worlds apart and "never the twain shall meet." But one day he discovers that the two friends behind the scenes were long closely connected with an unsuspected bond that was very unsettling.

When such a revelation comes, is it better to pick and choose or abandon both? The lesson of the Buddha's board is not to let yourself be paralyzed by the tendency to polarize, remaining oblivious to patterns of behavior, whether selfless or self-serving, that may change depending on circumstances and perspective. Sticking with labels fails to see the transitions and alternations between Fox and Buddha, that someone may seem deceptive in one context and supportive in another. As soon as you get locked into a set view, flexibility and agility are lost. The Japanese term for "supple," (*junan*) is a word whose meaning can range from compliance that verges on the obsequious to a kind of dynamic agility. It has the same root as *judo*, which is literally the "way of cotton" or the soft and elastic, "bend but don't break" way of overcoming barriers.

The Zen view is evoked in the famous film, *Rashomon*, directed by Akira Kurosawa. The film is set in medieval Japan and revolves around the murder of a nobleman and the alleged rape of his wife by a bandit who accosts them on a deserted forest road. The story is told from four different viewpoints. The wife, the bandit, a woodcutter who was an unseen witness to the incident, and the ghost of the murdered husband all present their versions of the events. As these four very different versions of the tale unfold, it becomes clear that there is no core of "truth" with respect to what happened. Instead, as a character in the film suggests, we are left with a succession of "lies." All of the versions have a common strand and a degree of credibility, yet each has elements that are misleading or false, whether intentionally or because of unintended bias or faulty perception. The film presents a narrative structure that is fragmented and distorted. There is no single standpoint or frame of reference to rely upon. It is up to the viewer to determine where reality lies.

The Buddha's board cannot help but obstruct and impede. For the Hermit, who realizes that there are so many perspectives that in the end every viewpoint is relative and ambiguous, the Buddha's board hinders the ability to discern and judge. Similarly, the Warrior cannot act if perception is clouded by uncertainty. Yet any attempt to force an Encounter without having drawn the right cards or knowing how to play those you have been dealt will have mixed or unsatisfactory results, or decline into a Confrontation, as in the home truth: Leverage is not something you really have until you really have it.

Fourth Side of the House

In traditional Buddhist lore, an accomplished master gains certain supranormal powers such as reading minds, seeing past and future karma, and overcoming bodily constraints to pass through walls or levitate. Although there is a legend about an enlightened person who gained so much wisdom that he sprouted an Eye on the Top of His Head, Zen has generally interpreted these capacities as symbols of inner discipline and control. As a master says,

- *My supranormal powers are carrying water and chopping wood.*

Everyday life is qualified by uncertainty, instability, and unpredictability. Even a Buddha who has escaped many basic elements of weakness and defilement is still a human with frailties, faults, foibles, flaws, and failures. In recognition of this condition, a requirement stipulated by Sakyamuni, the historical Buddha in India, instituted a system of fortnightly confessions for the assembly of monks that is still observed in Zen practice today.

This rite is directed to fellow monks rather than an abbot or father superior. Punishments are dictated not only by the seriousness of the sin (murder, theft, sexual indiscretion, and misusing supranormal powers are the worst offenses), but by the amount of time lapsed since the sin was committed. Delay in confessing allows the karma generated to linger rather than enabling the problem to be quickly redressed.

The Buddhist rite can degenerate into an overly formal, mechanical exercise but its significance is like the advice given to athletes and performers, whose every action is observed by both a general audience and peers:

- *Stay within yourself, recognize your limits and don't overstep your bounds. Do not force an opportunity, but wait for the right moment and then seize it.*

A learner, disciple, or trainee should try to work with the restrictions of self-perception in order to transcend and become free from them. Over- and underconfidence are deadly enemies.

In Zen, each aspect of experience has a twofold quality:

- *The double-edged sword has the capacity to take life and give back life.*

The image of the double-edged sword appears in both the Old Testament and the New Testament. In the Bible, this connotes twice the destructiveness, a double punishment for evil and wrongdoing. But in Zen's paradoxical discourse, the second edge has the opposite effect from the first one. By winning approval for a project you may lose out on another initiative. The very factor that gains an advantage creates the condition for detraction, and vice versa. As in colloquial English, the double-edged sword cuts both ways. When we call something a double-edged sword, it is to warn that some idea or proposed action will have a negative as well as a positive outcome.

The negative always accompanies the positive. Likewise, each cloud has a silver lining. An obstacle to knowledge may prove instructive or remedial. There are times when being out of the loop lends an advantage. Not knowing about a controversy among colleagues allows you to treat the respective parties with neutrality and impartiality. Maybe failure has done you a favor. If there are Pyrrhic victories, then there must be defeats that are a dignified loss that may well resemble winning because so much is gained in terms of knowledge or insight.

As a kid playing baseball in neighborhood playgrounds, Lefty Heine often thought to himself, "If I could only throw one pitch in one game in the major leagues, my life will be made." Later that season he saw his favorite pitcher, Robin Roberts, who was one of the greats of the era but past his prime, give up a gopher ball in the late innings of a crucial game. Yet the star player, yanked by the manager and with the boos of the crowd buzzing in his ears, managed to leave the mound that day without looking dejected or humiliated. A washed-up has-been? No way. He was more my hero than ever before.

This example of walking away from the scene seems quite different from the case of Kuei-shan kicking over the water pitcher, but in both examples the individual transcends the immediate situation with a lofty, noble perspective that transfixes and transforms everyone involved on the spot. Whether or not you are successful in the short run, maintaining dignity and integrity allows you to prevail in a subsequent phase.

You realize you have fallen short when an adversary, whose strength you have underestimated, forces an Encounter before you are ready. Or perhaps you are surprised by a development sprung at the eleventh hour by a newcomer's agenda. The basic mistake is to let pride or arrogance lead you to go outside your game or overstep your bounds. This leaves you oblivious and unresponsive to on-the-spot reversals or reprisals, or with a mind incapable of shifting gears. And if you resort to a nonrenewable, "scorched-earth" policy out of revenge or antipathy, you sacrifice dignity for a short-term gain.

Effective counterstrategies begin by recognizing at an early, preemptive stage that you are weaker than anticipated, so that you are ready to adapt and adjust at a moment's notice. If you are overwhelmed by someone else's agenda and unable to tell Buddha from Fox, remember from EPA not to respond on the basis of polarized feelings and to purify your reactions through an elevated level of intuition.

When bluffs are called and disguises unmasked, Daijobu Diplomacy results in a constructive realignment of the levels of consciousness. Switch from Nike's "Just Do It!" theology to the old-fashioned way of Avis rent-a-car, "We're No. 2. We try harder." This allows time to choose to withdraw or retreat, and you can later choose your battles … or create your Encounters.

Sometimes you may need to dig in by adopting the attitude of a real estate agent who once appeared in a show of the *Rhoda* TV series. Rhoda's boyfriend nixed a sure-thing deal on buying a house by making a series of unreasonable last-minute demands because, as it turned out, he was really trying to get out of their wedding plans. When it was clear the deal had fallen through, he realtor approached him with apparent disgust, saying she had never been so humiliated in all her life. Then she turned on a dime and concluded the conversation by saying,

- *And if you are ever in the market for another house, here's my card.*

At other times there are serendipitous discoveries like the **Fourth Side of the House.** One day a bunch of our kids' friends from the neighborhood descended on our home and when they left it seemed like every single thing was left out of place. Realizing that we could not find a favorite bike, we searched behind every bush in the front yard, the back yard, and by the driveway to the left of the house. Could they really have taken the bike away? Can no one be trusted?

A few days later, after having given up the search, one of the kids happened to take a little-used path along the side of the house we had forgotten to check because it backed right up against the house next door. The lost bike was there. We learned that you can never check things out too thoroughly and that there are always positive surprises in store along with the negatives. Similarly, Senpai understood from the Glass Suite episode that he needed to try to gain advantage from decline and turn adversity into opportunity.

According to Confucius, it takes time to develop a path of continuity and consistency:

- *At fifteen I set my heart on learning, at thirty I was established, at forty I had no perplexities, at fifty I understood the decrees of Heaven, at sixty my ear was in accord, and at seventy I followed what my heart desired but did not transgress what was right.*

Achieving a sense of accord and compatibility with principles of what is right and applying this in every situation is the goal of Zen.

In Kafka's *Before the Law* parable, the man from the country is kept waiting before the door of the law by the intimidating doorkeeper until it is too late and he is left to die. But according to Zen,

- *The Gateless Gate is easy to cross, because the gate is within you.*

Therefore,

- *Open wide both hands like someone who has nothing to lose.*

Isn't this just another way of speaking of freedom, the time for sprouting an eye on the top of the head?

Any day now, creative misreadings or misunderstandings of people or circumstance will bring you closer to truth, which is invariably mixed with untruth or the illusory. You can find this intertwining of positive and negative energies in,

- *Every grain of sand.*

Glossary/Index

Terms that are used in a special way in this book are designated by [WCZ]

Koan Translation

"Te-shan Carrying His Bundle"

Introduction

The *Blue Cliff Record* collection, with its elaborate use of rhetoric in multiple levels of commentaries proffered by two editors who lived a hundred years apart, is considered the peak composition in the classical koan tradition. There are several different styles included in the cases, which were first compiled along with a verse commentary in the eleventh century by Hsueh-tou and then given additional prose and verse commentary in the twelfth century by Yuan-wu. The styles include:

A. **Pointer** – brief introductory comments

B. **Main Case** narrative with **Capping Phrases** (ironic line-by-line commentaries)

C. **Verse Commentary** with **Capping Phrases**

The best procedure for reading the koan is to go through the entire passage in several stages. First, look over the pointer and read the narrative in bold script to get a sense of the story line of the main case. Then, reread each line of the case with capping phrases in italics to appreciate the way the nuances of the commentary are crucial for understanding the narrative. Finally study the verse with its own set of capping phrases.

The following is a complete translation of the pointer, narrative, verse, and capping phrases (note that additional prose commentary on the main case narrative is not included in this translation).

Translation

A. POINTER

Under the clear sky and bright sun, you don't have to point out this in the east or that in the west. But you still have to administer medicine appropriate to temporal conditions. Now tell me, in doing this is it better to release or to hold firm? To test this, consider the following case!

B. MAIN CASE (Bold) with
CAPPING PHRASES (*Italics*)

1. **Te-shan came to see Kuei-shan.**

   Look at him carrying a board on his shoulder. That wild fox spirit!

2. **He carried his bundle into the Dharma Hall.**

   This can't help but cause people to doubt him. He has already suffered his first defeat.

3. **Then he crossed from east side to west side, and again from west side to east side.**

   He possesses the power of Zen, but what good does it do him?

4. **He looked around and said, "No one is here. There's nothing here," and then he left.**

Give him 30 blows of the staff! His spirit reaches up to the heavens, but only a real lion cub can roar like a lion.

[He checked things out!]

What a mistake, after all.

5. But when Te-shan got to the gates of the temple he thought to himself, "I really should not be so crude."

Letting it all go, or taking it all in? At first too high and then too low. When you realize the error of your ways, you should try to correct them. But how many people are capable of doing this?

6. So he entered the Dharma Hall once again, with full ceremony, to greet the master.

He acts the same way as before. This must be his second defeat. Watch out!

7. Kuei-shan just sat there.

He's watching that fellow with steely eyes. It takes someone like this to grab a tiger by the whiskers.

8. Te-shan held up his training mat and said, "Teacher."

Switching heads and changing faces, he stirs up waves even though there is no wind.

9. Kuei-shan reached for his fly-whisk.

See what kind of person he is, setting his strategy in motion even while remaining in his tent. Nothing can stop him from cutting off tongues of everyone in the world.

10. Te-shan cried out, shook his sleeves, and abruptly left.

This is the understanding of a wild fox spirit. In one shout, he expressed the provisional and the real, the illuminative and the functional. Among all those who can grab onto the clouds and grasp at the mist, he alone is uniquely skilled.

[He checked things out!]

What a mistake, after all.

11. **Te-shan turned from the Dharma Hall, put on his straw sandals, and departed.**

    The landscape is charming, but the case is far from over. Te-shan kept the hat covering his head, but lost the shoes covering his feet. He's lost any chance he may have once had.

12. **That evening Kuei-shan asked the monk in charge of the Monks Hall, "Where is the newcomer who was with me earlier today?"**

    He lost his footing in the east and gave up following the trail in the west. His eyes are gazing to the southeast but his heart is in the northwest.

13. **The head monk said, "At that time he turned away from the Dharma Hall, put on his straw sandals, and departed."**

    The sacred tortoise is dragging its tail, and deserves 30 blows. How many blows to the back of the head does it take for him to get it?

14. **Kuei-shan said, "After this he will dwell on the summit of a peak all by himself, and build a hut where he scolds the Buddhas and reviles the Patriarchs.**

    Kuei-shan draws his bow after the thief has already fled. No patchrobed monk in all the world will be able to follow after Te-shan.

    [He adds frost to the snow.]

    What a mistake, after all.

C. VERSE COMMENTARY (Bold)
with CAPPING PHRASES (*Italics*)

1. **The first time it was said, "He checked things out,"**
    The words are still ringing in our ears. Then, gone.

2. **The second time he said, "He checked things out,"**
    These are two different koans.

3. **The third time he said, "He adds frost to the snow"—
    and with that, Te-shan fell flat on his face.**
    *These three remarks do not mean the same thing. And
    where was it that Te-shan fell?*

4. **Like the famed general entering behind enemy lines,**
    *Watch out! There is no need to strike at the general of a
    defeated army. He has already given up his life.*

5. **Then making a narrow escape,**
    He came back to life while in the midst of death.

6. **Te-shan sets off on a mad dash,**
    *He must think he is alone. He summoned the 36
    stratagems and used up the supranormal powers, but
    what good did it do him?*

7. **But is not left alone.**
    *The cat has the power to overtake the leopard. Kuei-
    shan pierced his nostrils.*

8. **Sitting amid the weeds on the summit of the solitary
    mountain peak—**
    *In the final analysis, piercing the nostrils is hardly
    something strange. But why is Te-shan sitting there
    amid the weeds?*

9. Lord have mercy!

*Do you understand? Two swords are cutting each other.
There are two or even three of them walking down the
ancient path, all singing and clapping in harmony.
Then, Strike!*

Summary of Themes

The following table is a summary of the commentaries focusing on the two fundamental paradigms. In referring to the three main characters of the narrative, the initials indicate "T" for Te-shan, "K" for Kuei-shan, and "M" for the monk in charge of the Monks Hall who has a brief exchange with the abbot.

Movable Mind (lacking Zen insight)

Pulling the bow after the thief has already fled
- Carries the board on his shoulder - T
- Wild fox spirit! - T
- Causes people to doubt - T
- Suffers first defeat - T
- Has power, but what good does it do? - T
- Give him 30 blows of the staff - T
- Only a real lion cub roars like a lion - T
- At first too high and then too low - T
- Who can correct the error of their ways? - T
- Acts the same, must be second defeat - T
- Keeps hat, but loses shoes - T
- Loses any chance he one had - T
- Lost his footing in the east and gave up following the trail in the west - K
- Sacred tortoise dragging its tail - M
- How many blows to the back of his head does it take for him to get the point? - M
- Draws bow after thief has fled - K
- Adds frost to snow - K
- Don't strike general of a defeated army - T
- Thinks he is alone - T
- What good are the "36 Strategems" and supranormal powers? - T
- Sitting among the weeds on solitary peak - T

Unmoving Mind (with Zen insight)

Setting the strategy in motion while remaining in the tent
- He checked things out - T
- Watching with steely eyes - K
- Grabs tiger by the whiskers - K
- Switching heads and changing faces - T
- Stirs up waves without wind - T
- In one shout expresses provisional and real - T
- Grabs clouds, grasps mist - T
- Cat has power over leopard - K
- Cuts off tongues of everyone - K
- Switching heads and changing faces - T
- Stirs up the waves even though there is no wind -T
- Sets strategy in motion - K
- Cuts off tongues of everyone - K
- Dwells on the summit of a mountain all by himself - T **(by K)**
- Builds a hut where he scolds the Buddha and reviles the
    Patriarchs - T **(by K)**
- Came back to life in the midst of death -T
- Cat has power to overcome leopard - K
- Pierced his nostrils - K
- Singing and clapping in harmony - T & K
